WORKFORCE 2040

Pathways to Prosperity

SAGAMORE PRESS

Indianapolis, Indiana

ISBN 9798991271622 (pbk)
ISBN 9798991271677 (ebk)
Library of Congress Control Number: 2024944942

Typeset in Palatino Linotype

CONTENTS

Foreword

"The best way to predict the future is to create it."
– Abraham Lincoln and Peter Drucker

While there seems to be uncertainty about who is the source of this quote – a 19th century president or a 20th century management consultant – there is little doubt about the enduring truth of these words. They ring especially true as we prepare for a time of economic disruption and opportunity. We know that Indiana and the nation stand at a pivotal moment and that our willingness to confront tectonic changes will determine state and personal prosperity.

It is with this thought in mind that Sagamore Institute decided to revive the Workforce Series (*Workforce 2000* and *Workforce 2020*) that was developed by Hudson Institute, the predecessor organization to Sagamore Institute. Both earlier initiatives successfully offered ideas about the employment landscape and challenged policymakers, employers, and citizens to prepare for the new economy.

While the policy and economic environments created in past decades have enabled Indiana to achieve success in attracting jobs and investments, they are not designed for a time of rapid and consequential change. Sagamore Institute's Workforce 2040 initiative provides Indiana's public, private and philanthropic decision-makers with independent and pragmatic analyses, strategic predictions and policy recommendations needed to position Indiana for economic growth. It equips leaders with a comprehensive understanding of the key forces, trends and technological advances that impact the future of the workforce, work and learning. Using this future-focused perspective, *Workforce 2040* clarifies which issues are most important and suggests leading solutions to address them.

Similar to the earlier workforce studies, *Workforce 2040* explores the likely costs and benefits associated with Indiana's collective response through a scenario-building process that integrates three options: inaction, measured adaptation and bold reform. While predicting workforce trends is central to *Workforce 2040*, the publication of this book is not the singular purpose of the initiative. In partnership with leading education, workforce and economic partners, *Workforce 2040* will provide adaptive and ongoing analysis to update the predictions and recommendations as the future unfolds and take advantage of digital tools to reach broader audiences.

Another distinguishing element of this project is that the content has been created by both Sagamore researchers and key external subject matter experts. While Sagamore is leading the effort, success will be measured by the continued engagement of partners who will be implementing agendas that address the predictions and recommendations.

Between now and 2040, the pace of technological change will require personal resiliency in the face of uncertainty and opportunity. More than ever, it will mean that employers, educators and policymakers will need to collaborate as the stewards of Indiana's economy. Are we creating the economy we want and the talent we need to get there? *Workforce 2040: Pathways to Prosperity* seeks to answer that question by providing both a forecast and roadmap for action.

ABOUT SAGAMORE INSTITUTE

Sagamore Institute was founded in 2004 as a heartland-based, action-oriented think tank. We operate a network of scholars, policy experts and innovators to advance solutions to the world's biggest problems. Our ideas travel in two directions: we move upstream to change policy and reform systems, and we travel downstream to put ideas to work via best practices to improve lives and the places we live. Sagamore's three pillars of action are focused on creating opportunity, ensuring national security and advancing civil society. *Workforce 2040: Pathways to Prosperity* examines key workforce trends that impact all three areas and that challenge our state's economy and by extension the Midwest and the Nation.

Acknowledgements

In developing *Workforce 2040*, Sagamore Institute has benefited from the counsel of a group of individuals and organizations that have provided leadership, research and valuable insights. These advisers assisted Sagamore's staff, led by President Teresa Lubbers, Project Director Jacob Baldwin and Senior Advisor Bret Swanson, in guiding the project throughout the months leading up to its publication.

An Advisory Group that led the design and set priorities consisted of Carol D'Amico, Neil Pickett, David Shane, Carol Rogers, Claudia Cummings and Ryan Kitchell. Key partner organizations joined as financial and content contributors, including the Indiana Chamber of Commerce, Central Indiana Corporate Partnership, Ascend Indiana, TechPoint, AgriNovus Indiana, Biocrossroads, Conexus Indiana, Elevate Ventures, the Indiana Governor's Workforce Cabinet, Indiana Economic Development Corporation, INvestED, Strada Education Foundation, Lumina Foundation, One America Financial, Arnold Ventures, Purdue University and TPMA. Tim Swarens, Emily Schmicker and Erin Darling contributed their copyediting, cover design and publication expertise, respectively. Special thanks are extended to the authors of *Workforce 2040*, as named in each chapter.

The research, predictions and recommendations included in *Workforce 2040* were provided by the authors and the organizations they represent. The project is not concluded with the publication of this book. Now, the work continues as we revise predictions and implement recommendations throughout the years leading to 2040.

Teresa Lubbers, Sagamore President
Jacob Baldwin, Project Director

Indianapolis, Indiana
September 2024

Executive Summary

While 2040 seems to be far away, it's clear now the changes that lead up to that time are far-reaching and demand attention and preparation. Some may think that this moment is no different than previous times of economic upheaval, but others predict the coming years will bring seismic pressures and opportunities far greater than previous ones. *Workforce 2040: Pathways to Prosperity* is designed to analyze current workforce trends, predict new realities, and offer actionable recommendations.

The book is organized around three key areas: *the future of the workforce; the future of work; and the future of learning.* In partnership with key workforce, education and business leaders and through an Indiana lens, it explores seven key trends that will shape the future of work:

- **The 21st century demographic cliff** – Indiana will experience slow to almost no population growth as we move to 2040 and beyond. This slowing growth will translate into increasingly and historically smaller gains in the labor force, especially in the highly sought-after prime working and household formation ages of 25 to 54. Fierce national competition for skilled workers will require a laser focus buttressed by creative strategies for building, attracting and retaining talent.

- **Entrepreneurial and innovative firms will hollow out complacent ones** - To drive economic success, it will be essential to develop a thriving innovation ecosystem and capitalize on high-growth, high-potential firms and intentionally grow more of them into medium and large enterprises. High-growth firms generate more jobs than older firms and attract high-skilled talent. A defensive posture against a changing world must be replaced with a focus on building as dynamic and agile an economy as possible.

- **Technology takeover** - Technology demonstrably affects wage and income growth for workers. Transitioning an ever-increasing number of workers into more productive industries with better use of technology should be a chief objective of any workforce policy.

1

Artificial intelligence will rewire every sphere – from the arts to investments. Indiana leaders should plan for a future where jobs that are eliminated are replaced with ones that are more productive and meaningful.

- **Unequal opportunity for personal prosperity based on education and training** – As jobs are created and eliminated in the new economy, individuals are at risk of not being prepared for changing job roles and related job skills. This risk will translate into groups of people who could be left behind, driving income disparity and social stratification. From an individual standpoint, people must be equipped with the resiliency to tackle new challenges. Likewise, employers cannot sit on the sidelines expecting that their talent needs will be met but rather must be committed to training and equipping their employees.

- **A manufacturing renaissance that is favoring the onshoring of many critical products** – After a long period of globalization that saw many raw materials and components outsourced to overseas facilities, many companies are rethinking their supply chain strategies. A rapidly changing labor market, supply chain disruptions, and a technological revolution make onshoring more attractive. At the same time, being globally competitive will be essential to accruing the benefits of exporting and access to global supply chains.

- **A more employee-centered system will emerge** – As employers search for qualified employees, as the youth population shrinks, and work becomes less place-bound, individuals will have greater leverage in the labor market and their preferences for quality of place will matter more. If the "work from anywhere" shift continues, as much evidence suggests that it will, then competition among communities to provide affordable housing, quality education, safety, and a robust, welcoming community culture will matter more. Equally critical, employers will need to ensure workplaces meet these expectations.

- **The future of learning will be defined by a greater demand for alignment between learning and work** – For both learners and employers, there is a growing desire for learning experiences that position individuals for employment and workplace mobility. In addition, there is a practical recognition that learning will be more personalized, lifelong, and provided in both formal and informal settings.

The implications of these trends are explored in Chapters 1 through 9. Chapter 10 includes predictions, recommendations and necessary actions to ensure that we shape the economy we want. ∎

1

Riding the Wave: Accelerating into the AI Era

By Bret Swanson
Entropy Economics

Who would have predicted more than 60 percent of today's jobs are in roles that didn't exist in 1940? In 1850, agriculture accounted for nearly 60 percent of American jobs. By 1950, that portion had fallen to just 15 percent. And today it's just around 2 percent. Over that same period, U.S. manufacturing employment rose from around 12 percent to 25 percent and then fell again, back to 12 percent.

Jarring technological transformations in artificial intelligence, robots, and biology will soon generate unimagined wealth and opportunity. But workers, firms, and states who are unprepared or complacent could fall even further behind than they are today.

How will existing jobs change? What are the jobs of the future? Matching the future economy's demands with a robust supply of talent and skills is a big part of the equation. Retraining and lifelong learning – both formal and informal – play an important role. Any attempt to merely accommodate onrushing disruptions, however, is bound to fall short. As Yogi Bera said, "It's tough to make predictions – especially about the future." Indiana's strategy, therefore, must rely on a proactive corollary: The easiest way to predict the future is to build it.

Over the past three decades, three major shifts dominated the U.S. economic landscape:

(1) Information technology propelled an explosion of wealth, if not always job numbers, in technology and finance. Lots of talent migrated to the American coasts.

(2) Global manufacturing shifted to southeast Asia. For Indiana, a historic strength in manufacturing turned to relative weakness when information technology and globalization induced a rapid reorientation of the U.S. economy.

(3) Health, education, and services generated large gains in job numbers but not incomes. These sectors tend toward low productivity growth and thus low wage growth. And yet too much of Indiana's economy is concentrated in these mostly local industries.

Today, some of the trends are intensifying, others reversing. Information technology is poised for its next chapter – the artificial intelligence acceleration. Globalization, on the other hand, is in retreat. Will a new bipartisan skepticism of China lead to an American industrial renaissance – or a dangerous retrenchment from world trade? Meanwhile, healthcare spending is poised to swiftly pass 20 percent of GDP, potentially generating lots of jobs to serve an aging population – but also swamping state, local, federal, and company budgets.

In this chapter, we focus on technology. More than any other factor, it drives economies and thus history. The wheel, the printing press, the steam engine; automobiles and airplanes; lasers, microchips, and now AI.

INDIANA IN 2024

First, however, let's briefly consider the present. Prudent leadership over the past two decades has put Indiana on sounder financial footing than most of its Midwestern neighbors. While some states pushed away business and shed population, Indiana attracted new residents and investment.

This modest outperformance of struggling peers, however, will not be nearly good enough in the next 20 years. Indiana has weathered the downsides of globalization, supplied efficient government services, and contained living costs (save health care) better than many. But we've not fully leveraged the power of entrepreneurship, the internet, or other breakthrough technologies. Indiana is a great place to live and raise families; yet our economy remains far too concentrated in low-productivity, low-wage sectors.

Booming peer cities like Charlotte, Nashville, and Denver highlight the challenge and possibilities for Indianapolis. Over the last 15 years, these three peers generated new jobs in high-income sectors such as finance and technology at rates 50 percent to 200 percent faster than Indianapolis and a fifth peer, Columbus, Ohio. Indianapolis compares favorably to the others in affordability but matches only Columbus in most of the crucial growth and income factors.

New research by economist Philip Powell, an Indiana University professor and director of the Indiana Business Research Center, provides a jolting reality check for the Indiana economy. Among Indianapolis' 20 most abundant occupations relative to other metro areas, only three pay more than the national average wage – physicians, health educators, and financial specialists (due largely to payroll clerks at the Defense Finance Accounting Service headquarters).

These metro data fairly reflect Indiana's economy as a whole. Most of Indiana's highest paying jobs are concentrated in local, non-scalable work such as health care, education, and law. These are worthy professions. But every region has them, and they don't often grow much faster than the population. A region that sells mostly local services to itself cannot generate the kind of explosively growing firms nor attract the diverse talent necessary to fuel an upward economic spiral.

The true vibrancy of a regional economy is determined by high-value exports to other regions, often based on scalable ideas. Today, that means software, energy, advanced materials, financial products, pharmaceuticals, complex manufactured goods, digital content, and technical services.

Warsaw, Indiana's success as a biomedical hub is an example of tech-based scale. Other Hoosier cities and regions – Fort Wayne, West Lafayette, Bloomington, Evansville – are generating momentum in this direction.

Our challenge is to encourage these leaders and expand similar efforts around the state.

THE CHALLENGE OF SCALE

To date, information technologies are the most scalable of all. The internet allows companies to quickly reach billion-person markets and trillion-dollar valuations. Now, AI is poised to scale products, companies, and many people in unprecedented and unpredictable ways.

Technologists have dreamt of AI since at least the early 1950s. After many fits and starts over the decades, the dream finally seemed close at hand when OpenAI delivered ChatGPT in late 2022. Everyone immediately saw it was a quantum leap.

Figure 1-1. GPT-4 matches human performance on many advanced exams

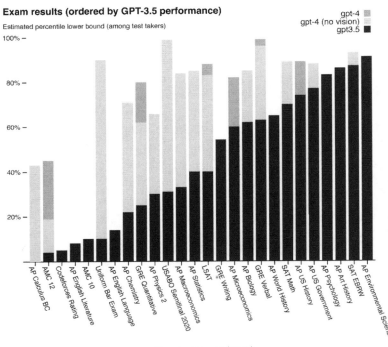

Source: OpenAI (2023).

Standardized tests provided eye-popping evidence of AI's new capabilities. As you can see in Figure 1-1 nearby, OpenAI's GPT-4 model scored in the 80th to 90th percentiles on many diverse exams, from AP biology and physics to the LSAT and bar exam. The Claude 3.5 model from Anthropic appears to beat even GPT-4's impressive results. Like all general-purpose technologies, artificial intelligence will both render millions of tasks and jobs obsolete and also generate millions of new jobs, often in entirely new categories.[1] Single-person start-ups might be common.

Pessimists focus on obsolescence. But AI could reverse the knowledge economy trend that punished workers not expert in science, law, finance, or information technology. People whose natural talents don't include, say, computers or writing may find AI supercharges the skills they do possess but which they were previously unable to scale.

New research shows ChatGPT, for example, helps poor writers 40 percent more than excellent writers. Moreover, AI itself will tutor and train un- or underemployed workers for new jobs far better than previous re-skilling programs. MIT economist David Autor optimistically suggests AI could lead to a middle-class renaissance.[2]

The unique opportunity that AI offers humanity is to push back against the process started by computerization – to extend the relevance, reach and value of human expertise to a larger set of workers. Because artificial intelligence can weave information and rules with acquired experience to support decision-making, it can enable a larger set of workers equipped with necessary foundational training to perform higher-stakes decision-making tasks currently arrogated to elite experts, such as doctors, lawyers, software engineers and college professors. In essence, AI – used well – can assist with restoring the middle-skill, middle-class heart of the U.S. labor market that has been hollowed out by automation and globalization. Some have suggested AI could even lead to a liberal arts renaissance too.

Scalability does not mean every company or individual has to seek out maximum ambition and market size. The very scale of the opportunity means that millions of niches will also open up for creative companies, entrepreneurs, and workers to leverage the new tools, often in entirely new product categories. Small companies will disrupt today's monopolies, whose large scale is often an illusion not of innovation but intransigence and inefficiency. As technology hoovers up value from unproductive tasks, creative companies will hollow out complacent ones. The key is to be the former, not the latter.

THE NEW INFORMATION INFRASTRUCTURE

To grasp the magnitude of the AI boom, consider the sudden leap of computer chip firm Nvidia. In the space of a few years, Nvidia exploded from relative unknown to, briefly, the world's most valuable company. Between the first quarter of 2023 and the first quarter of 2024, Nvidia sales of its AI chips quintupled from just under $5 billion to nearly $25 billion. As of July 2024, the company was worth $3.3 trillion, just slightly less than Apple and Microsoft, but more than Google and Amazon.

Nvidia was perfectly positioned for AI's new computing architecture, which required highly parallel processors. As the principle of Moore's law began to run out of steam on microprocessors (CPUs), Nvidia's graphics processors (GPUs) and other highly parallel chips took up the lofty exponential expectation.[3] The buildout of the AI computing infrastructure is now well underway. It will rival and may surpass the cost of building the Internet. Between 1996 and 2023, U.S. communications firms invested more than $2.5 trillion on cross-country fiber optic lines, mobile antennas and towers, switches, routers, and broadband links to homes and offices. We also invested hundreds of billions more in giant cloud-computing warehouses, which stored our data and powered millions of webpages, streams, feeds, and apps. This total rewiring of our communications infrastructure transformed the economy and society.

Now, AI computing is shifting data center infrastructure into an even higher gear. To generate everything from artificial images to machine-written essays, the AI companies must first train "models" with exabytes of data culled from all historical Internet content. In 2024, a leading-edge AI training cluster consisting of 100,000 chips might consume 100 megawatts of electricity, or enough to power 100,000 homes. By 2026, one AI training warehouse might contain one million chips and consume one gigawatt, or the capacity of a large nuclear reactor.

Training an AI model, however, is only the beginning. The second half of the equation is "inference" – or querying the models to generate answers to our questions and commands. Delivering the services you and I want – reading, digesting, answering, and learning from our requests – will require yet more computation and power. One analyst predicts that by 2030, at least four of the large AI companies will each build a training cluster with 100 million chips, costing $1 trillion, and consuming 100 gigawatts, or 20 percent of current U.S. electricity production.[4] Such a projection may seem wildly implausible. Surely, today's overexuberant AI boom will by that time go bust. Supply will outpace demand; financing will dry up.[5] Or perhaps it will run into resource constraints – materials, power, construction workers.

Skeptics will correctly warn that the early internet building boom was violently interrupted by the tech crash of 2000-01. Hundreds of dot-com firms and dozens of large fiber-optic networks and broadband equipment companies went bankrupt. Nearly 25 years later, however, the temporary overeagerness and financial losses of the late 1990s and early 2000s look mild compared to the size and influence of today's internet economy. After a major stumble, the $3-trillion network and cloud-computing foundation propelled the mobile, app, software-as-a-service, and new media revolutions, with seemingly limitless video streams and podcasts fundamentally altering all entertainment, news, and commentary.

In the same way, the new multi-trillion-dollar AI infrastructure will unlock hundreds of companies and thousands of new applications across every industry, old and new, while generating a content tsunami even larger and more diverse than today's internet giants like Netflix, YouTube, and Spotify. Venture capitalist Marc Andreessen speculates about entirely new content categories, such as "massively multiplayer dreams."

Despite Nvidia's spectacular technology and well-deserved plaudits, the current GPU architectures, like CPUs before them, will run out of steam. We need to invent faster and far more energy efficient computing substrates and architectures, making today's mind-numbingly infeasible dollar and energy projections more achievable.[6] Graphene is especially promising as a substrate, and a return to analog computing may be the only way to surmount the trillion-dollar data center obstacle.

THE PRODUCTIVITY GAP

Technology is no mere toy. It affects wage and income growth for workers whose firms deploy it most aggressively and use it most creatively. In a 2017 study, Michael Mandel and I found a yawning productivity gap between firms that use lots of information technology and those that do not.[7] Productivity in the "digital industries," we found, grew at a robust 2.7-percent annual rate over the previous 15 years. But productivity growth in the "physical industries" plummeted, to just 0.7 percent per year.

A significant portion of this differential could be explained by the industries' huge differential investments in – and creative use of – information technology. The physical industries at the time accounted for around 70 percent of U.S. output and 74 percent of employment but made just 30 percent of the investments in infotech.

This "information gap" may help explain the large pay divergence. At the end of 2016, average total compensation for the 90.5 million workers in the physical industries was $55,600. But total compensation for the 32.6 million workers in the digital industries averaged $92,000. Digital employees thus account for 26 percent of the private sector workforce but earn 37 percent of total pay. It's not just because of a few high-paid executives in Silicon Valley and Wall Street.

In separate work, Mandel found that wage premiums for mid-skill occupations in digital versus physical industries range from 15 percent to 38 percent.[8] For example, sales representatives in digital firms earn 15 percent more than non-digital sales reps. Workers in advanced distribution centers, such as Amazon's high-tech warehouses, earn 31 percent more than retail workers in the same geographic area. This tends to support the conclusions that productivity and pay are still linked, and technology differentials are a big part of the explanation.

Yes, skills matter. But regardless of skill level, moving more workers into more productive industries with more and better use of technology should be a chief objective of any workforce policy. TechPoint, Indiana's chief promoter of technology acceleration, is helping the cause through its Mission 41K effort, "a collaborative movement to address the largest problem tech employers are facing today – finding, hiring and retaining qualified tech talent."[9]

Today's projections for an AI productivity boom are all over the map. Some believe gains will be modest, perhaps bumping annual growth from a paltry 1 percent to a much better 2 or 3 percent. Others predict a "singularity," in which superintelligent machines invent more superintelligent machines, producing unlimited innovation. Bridgewater Associates, the world's largest hedge fund, has surveyed the highly variable productivity research and believes productivity gains will be real but not unprecedentedly large: "We think full-blown explosive growth is unlikely."[10]

Even short of economic nirvana, AI's radically deflationary effects will revolutionize specific tasks, jobs, firms, and industries. As Bridgewater reminds us:

> *The marginal cost of a given product falling to zero can be either a best-case or worst-case scenario for its sellers, depending on their pricing power. We saw this in the case of the IT revolution of the 1990s and 2000s, which brought the marginal cost of production or distribution to zero for many businesses involved in creating and disseminating information. Besides consumers, who benefited from a profusion of free and low-cost products, the "winners" included software companies that earned eye-popping margins by charging a premium for products that cost nothing to distribute. The "losers" (such as newspaper publishers and camera companies) could not compete with zero on a marginal-cost basis; they shrunk dramatically as consumers opted for much cheaper (often free) alternatives.[11]*

WEALTH AND WORRY

AI will be like computing is today – everywhere, embedded in everything we do. It will rewire every sphere, from the arts to investments. One of the first things the new software is transforming is the building of software itself. AI will turn lots of people into "software developers" even if they don't know it. Amjad Masad, the CEO of Replit, argues that adding Chat-GPT-like features to his own company's software tools boosts the productivity of his "10x engineers" – elite developers – by 30 to 50 percent. That's a huge improvement. Yet it may provide an even bigger boost to novices – improving their ability to "write" code (often by just narrating what they want the AI to do) by a nearly infinite amount.

As the personal computer expanded computer accessibility to tens of millions of regular people, beyond the mere thousands of scientists who used them in university research labs, these new AI tools will also expand software, apps, and content generation to non-technical people. Indeed, software development may fade into the background of what everyone does, the way the iPhone touch screen allows anyone to manipulate a computer unconsciously. Of course, building the new tools that expand the user-friendliness of AI systems will still largely be the province of elite technicians. But the entire stack and value chain will have moved upward.

As AI empowers millions of people to do extraordinary things, it could also wipe out giant swaths of existing tasks and jobs, from office workers to vehicle drivers. Some have argued that where previous innovations in information technology automated lower-skilled jobs and benefited highly skilled workers, AI may automate many of those high-skilled jobs as well. Nick Bostrom, author of *Superintelligence,* believes AI and automation will lead to "full unemployment." Even Elon Musk, an AI enthusiast, believes "there will come a point when no job is needed."[12] Musk, however, makes an important caveat: "You can have a job if you want to have a job, for sort of personal satisfaction. But the AI will be able to do everything."[13] Musk's prophecy of unimaginable abundance and luxury jobs is still a dream well into the future. (Or perhaps it's a nightmare. He believes abundance may cause a crisis of meaning.) And yet it contains an important grain of truth for the nearer term.

In other words, AI could generate enough wealth in the productive and creative sectors that it helps pay for a realignment of people into new, more productive, more meaningful jobs. Or perhaps it allows people to reprioritize their lives – say, in a modest shift away from the modern necessity of dual income families. It might also be argued that a significant portion of today's jobs are superfluous. These jobs are often embedded in legacy industries or even modern tech monopolies, both of which face too little competition. Unproductive jobs can be found in government, but in truth every firm and industry has them. They are all cost. They do not exist for purely economic reasons. Call them fake jobs.

One potential scenario is that AI advances so radically and heightens the gap between productive and unproductive jobs so clearly that superfluous employment can no longer be justified. A big policy question then arises. Will we *allow* massive productivity gains to occur? Or will we protect bloated firms, industries, and agencies with the stated objective of "saving jobs"? There's a real question whether productivity gains in some sectors – such as healthcare and education – are feasible or even legal. In other words, automation can't eliminate fake jobs. True productivity and thus income gains require pain. Economist F.A. Hayek called it creative destruction for a reason.

SUPERINTELLIGENCE?

Like previous generations of computing, AI is vastly superior to humans in many respects. Seventy years ago, the first computers performed basic arithmetic faster than human "computers" with pencil and paper, which is where the term originated. Today, they often exceed us in memory, pattern matching, and hundreds of specific tasks.

And yet the search for artificial general intelligence, or AGI, in which a machine emulates every facet of human capacity is still out of reach. Yes, predictions of AGI have drawn nearer in recent years. Some now say we will "achieve AGI" as soon as 2027. But "achieving AGI" is nearly impossible to define. As AI matches or exceeds more and more discrete human abilities, we learn just how special is the human mix of sense, perception, intuition, logic, physical agility, interaction, adaptation, motivation, and creativity. Biology continues to wow us with its still little-understood depth.

The human advantage is especially clear on the metric of energy efficiency. We simultaneously do amazingly versatile things, both conscious and unconscious, with very few calories compared to computers. Think back to one of the great AI breakthroughs of the last decade. In 2016, Google's Deepmind shocked the world when its new AI program, AlphaGo, defeated the great Lee Sodol at the board game of Go. It had been nearly 20 years since IBM's DeepBlue beat Gary Kasparov in chess, and Go far exceeds chess in complexity and strategy. AGI surely was now just around the corner.

Not so fast. AlphaGo was still a single-purpose machine. It played a well-defined game with clear rules and a limited playing field. It could not generate images or write essays. And the energy differential was enormous. A human brain consumes around 20 watts of power. AlphaGo, on the other hand, consisted of 2,200 computer chips consuming around one megawatt of power – 50,000 times more than its human Go opponent! A brain, moreover, had a million times more synaptic connections than the best artificial neural network at the time – thus giving humans something like 50 billion times the general-purpose hardware per watt.

Since then, the computing and algorithmic advances of large language models (LLMs) have partially closed that gap. They are both more powerful and far more agile across a wider range of tasks. Yet the human brain is still around one million times more energy efficient than today's best neural networks. One reason innovation in the physical economy has lagged the digital economy is that people, objects, and natural environments are more difficult to computerize than numbers, text, and photos. Humans still excel in physical space. Humanoid robots and self-driving cars are making real progress. But the economic crossover points have come far slower than in natively information-intensive arenas – for example, financial services or video content.

The bottom line is that AI will in coming years match and exceed humans at many cognitive and even physical tasks. But our magical mix of biological hardware and software still towers over machines in important ways. Nowhere is this clearer than in what we call "creativity," perhaps the most profound of all human traits. And this is where AI skeptics make their stand. As smart as computers are, they will never anytime soon be creative. Computers are built to obey. We tell them to add, subtract, and multiply. Given a known input, we can predict the output.

Not so with LLMs, backers of superintelligence reply. For the first time, we have truly probabilistic computing. Ask an LLM the same question twice, and it may return different answers. It may even deliver fake citations, illogical ramblings, or pure nonsense. Engineers call these "hallucinations." Hallucinations are maddening when we want hard facts. But they may be necessary if AI is ever to approach something like "creativity." True creativity is unpredictable. Regular computers were designed and built to be absolutely predictable. Obedient, in other words.

Creativity requires just the opposite. Art, innovation, and scientific discovery require outside-the-box thinking. Or as physicist David Deutsch puts it, disobedience is a prerequisite for true creativity. Can disobedient computers lead to creativity? The first steps toward creativity are already seen, but they are mostly hybrid. Let the AI brainstorm, while humans select the best ideas. The bottom line is that humans are still in charge. The most likely path over the next few decades will be intense human-machine cooperation, not relegation of humans to irrelevance.

POLICY IDEAS

The most productive ways to avoid or mitigate the downsides of technological disruption are to promote robust growth, rapid technological adoption, continuous education, strong families and communities, and flexible, adaptable labor markets. Entrepreneurship and economic growth generate new paths for those displaced. Wealth and strong communities provide resources to better take care of those who do fall between the cracks – and to help them rebound. Continuous education and re-skilling can reduce the time spent un- or underemployed. High quality education and healthy cultural habits help build resilient citizens.

Historically, continuing education and workforce re-skilling programs generated mixed results, at best. These top-down efforts often suffered from too much bureaucracy and an inability to predict the future. A more individualized, bottom-up approach may be far better suited to today's more diverse and fast-changing economy.

- Indiana should consider expanding Career Scholarship Accounts, flexible state grants that individuals can deploy across a wider range of educational and training platforms. Personalized skill development vehicles like CSAs offer a highly customizable complement to more traditional state financial aid programs and employer-sponsored training opportunities. Instead of top-down predictions of what every worker should train for, CSAs provide an agile bottom-up path for both workers and providers of education and training. With individuals deciding when and how to deploy these flexible dollars, a more diverse and innovative array of educational content and delivery channels should arise to meet personalized needs. Better incentives should better match workers with educational services. Providers competing for CSA dollars will likely adapt to real-world market signals at a much faster pace than a bureaucracy's out-of-date design.

- Support collaborative efforts to build Indiana's pool of technology talent, such as TechPoint's Mission 41K.

- Energy will be a crucial foundation of every industry and job, from advanced manufacturing to AI. Indiana should prioritize low-cost energy abundance.

- Prioritize entrepreneurship, especially in scalable, high-productivity industries instead of the mostly non-scalable, local industries that dominate today.

- Ride the wave, don't cower from it. Rapid adoption of new technologies in existing and entrepreneurial firms is the best way to avoid disruption and displacement.

Avoiding or blocking AI is the surest way to get crushed by it. Many states, for example, are proposing highly restrictive AI laws. They fear it might be used in dangerous ways or it might destroy jobs. But such policies are likely to boomerang. Every technology can be misused or even deployed for illegal purposes. In general, existing laws and principles should be used to combat harmful acts, such as fraud, which happen to employ AI. Punish the criminal act, but do not preempt the general use of AI, which will have endless benefits.

States that restrict AI will have difficulty achieving their policy goals. Like the internet, AI will be everywhere, undeterred by physical borders. One sure way to lose economically would be to restrict AI at home, only for voracious AI firms and apps originating elsewhere to hollow out your own firms and industries.

Instead, we should *adjust* our legal tools and institutions to encourage healthy *adaptation* to the AI world. The CSAs mentioned above are one example of an adaptive approach. Another example: a new AI content explosion may dwarf the swirl of social media which consumes teenage (and non-teenage) brains. Instead of outright bans, however, we might encourage technological tools and new cultural norms to help protect people from the attention-sapping effects and deceptions of a new content tsunami.

AN ENTREPRENEURIAL ACCELERATION

Phillip Powell, the economist at Indiana University, argues that "high-skilled creative talent is the main driver of economic success." But education and training are only half the story. Why are low- and middle-income Americans so much better off than their counterparts in highly educated Europe? In large part it is because the U.S. produces six times more billion-dollar startups than Europe. These explosive firms deliver the productivity gains and wealth that make even our less innovative industries and workers richer.

Indiana may educate more bio-tech geniuses, mechanical engineers, software developers, and financial quants. If it doesn't have innovative firms for them to join, however, or provide the entrepreneurial sandbox where they can start their own companies, they will go where their unique skills are valued. Without top-line growth in Indiana, thousands of good jobs in construction, transportation, and support services will never happen.

Remote work will amplify and scramble the location equation. Working from anywhere paradoxically makes place both less and more important. No longer tied to their employers' central offices, many workers will even more strongly prioritize affordability, education, infrastructure, amenities, safety, and community.

An optimist might like Indiana's chances to build successfully upon its livability advantages. Likewise, entrepreneurial Indiana employers can leverage the talent of the world. On the other hand, if Indiana is complacent, its vulnerability to regions with better weather and more attractive work and life ecosystems could intensify.

All these factors only reinforce our thesis. Instead of playing defense against a changing world, we should aggressively build more high-growth, high potential firms and economic networks. This is the best way to shape the character of work, lift the overall trajectory of the economy, attract creative talent, and ride rather than cower from the inevitable waves of the AI acceleration. ∎

ABOUT ENTROPY ECONOMICS

Bret Swanson is president of Entropy Economics LLC, a technology research firm serving investors and technology companies. He is also a senior fellow at the National Center for Energy Analytics and a visiting fellow at the Krach Institute for Tech Diplomacy at Purdue. From 2009 to 2024, he was a trustee and chairman of the Indiana Public Retirement System (INPRS). Find his "Infonomena" newsletter and podcast at infonomena.substack.com.

CHAPTER NOTES

[1] For a good look at how the new LLMs are "general purpose technologies," see Tyna Eloundou, Sam Manning, Pamela Mishkin, and Daniel Rock. GPTs are GPTs: An Early Look at the Labor Market Impact Potential of Large Language Models. August 22, 2023. https://arxiv.org/pdf/2303.10130.

[2] David Autor. "How A.I. Could Help Rebuild the Middle Class." Noema. February 12, 2024. https://www.noemamag.com/how-ai-could-help-rebuild-the-middle-class/.

[3] See, for example, Bret Swanson. "Moore's Law at 50." American Enterprise Institute. 2015. https://www.aei.org/wp-content/uploads/2015/11/Moores-law-at-50.pdf. "The solution was found in parallelism. The rate of improvement in single-processor performance had indeed slowed a bit. But as clock speeds and voltages leveled off, firms began putting two, then four, then more processors on each chip, and the results were encouraging. This 'multicore' strategy was new to microprocessors, or CPUs, but it was already familiar in other types of chips that specialize in real-time processing of high-speed data, such as graphics processors (GPUs)…"

[4] Leopold Aschenbrenner. In section IIIa. Racing to the Trillion Dollar Cluster. Situational Awareness: The Decade Ahead. June 2024. https://situational-awareness.ai.

[5] Already, financial and venture firms are warning of an A.I. bubble. See, for example, analysis from Goldman Sachs (Gen AI: Too Much Spend, Too Little Benefit?" https://www.goldmansachs.com/intelligence/pages/gs-research/gen-ai-too-much-spend-too-little-benefit/report.pdf) and Sequoia Capital ("A.I.'s $600 billion question." https://www.sequoiacap.com/article/ais-600b-question/).

[6] See, for example, upstart chip companies such as Groq, Cerebras, and Extropic, which are building new computing architectures; and new materials advances, especially in graphene.

[7] Michael Mandel and Bret Swanson. The Coming Productivity Boom: Transforming the Physical Economy with Information. March 2017. http://entropyeconomics.com/wp-

CHAPTER NOTES (cont.)

content/uploads/2017/03/The-Coming-Productivity-Boom-Transforming-the-Physical-Economy-with-Information-March-2017.pdf.

[8] Michael Mandel. An Analysis of Job and Wage Growth in the Tech and Telecom Sector. Progressive Policy Institute. September 2017. www.progressivepolicy.org/wp-content/uploads/2017/09/PPI_TechTelecomJobs_V4.pdf.

[9] "Technology Talent and Workforce Mission41K Impact Network." Techpoint. Accessed July 2024. https://techpoint.org/talent-impact/.

[10] See Bridgewater Associates' numerous analyses of A.I.'s economic potential; for example, "Are We on the Brink of an AI Investment Arms Race?" "Assessing the Implications of a Productivity Miracle." "Exploring How AI Will Impact the Economy."

[11] Greg Jensen, Lauren Simon, and Josh Moriarity. "Assessing the Implications of a Productivity Miracle." Bridgewater Associates. November 30, 2023.

[12] Bloomberg Quicktakes. Video of Elon Musk. November 2, 2023. https://www.youtube.com/watch?v=HbiyTZae61A.

[13] Bloomberg Quicktakes. Elon Musk.

2

The 21st Century Demographic Cliff

By Carol Rogers with Matt Kinghorn
Indiana Business Research Center[†]

A region's economy thrives or dives because of the people who choose to live there. It is essential to monitor changes in the size and movement of our population. It is the fundamental barometer of a state, county, or region since it presages lackluster business or talent attraction.

What Indiana is facing now as we look to 2040 and beyond: very slow to almost no growth. This slowing growth, beginning between 1990 and 2000, will slow to a trickle by the 2040s. Indiana's population growth decade-by-decade will be measured in five figures instead of six figures. We will add less than 1,000 new Hoosiers a year between 2040 and 2050. The only time Indiana experienced such minimal growth was the 1980s, when the state experienced unprecedented out-migration and lower birth rates. Will the 2040s be the new 1980s? Are we at the demographic cliff or have we already begun to fall? The answer will be yes, unless.

[††] Written by Carol Rogers using the IBRC's latest official Indiana and county population and labor force projections, as of June 2024, produced by Matt Kinghorn. All tables, charts and maps in this chapter are from this source, unless otherwise noted.

The IBRC's projections are based on demographic data and provide a clear view of Indiana's potential future *if* past trends continue. It's important to note that these figures do not consider future economic conditions or land use decisions, which can be highly volatile or speculative. State policy will play a significant role in shaping businesses and residents' decisions to come to, stay in, or leave Indiana, underscoring the importance of thoughtful policy decisions. Further, certain population dynamics, such as migration, can be challenging to project. These dynamics are often susceptible to sudden shifts due to national and state policy.

Unless we succeed at attracting new people and especially young people seeking career opportunities and a great place to start and raise their families.

This picture isn't meant to be alarmist, but it should be sobering. It should be used to understand why Indiana needs a vision coupled with smart policies that create the environment to attract people to live and work here. Indiana is within a five-hour driving radius of more than 55 million people. Can Indiana convince some of them to move their households and businesses here? Answers to that question are threaded through this book, but for now let's focus on where we see our population and workforce numbers headed over the next 30 years.

Figure 2-1. 150 years of Indiana population growth

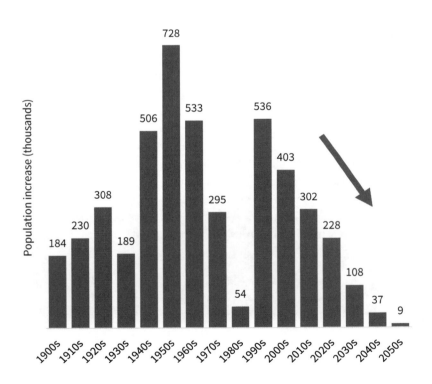

The demographic cliff can be attributed almost solely to our losses of young people ages 16 to 24. As Figure 2-2 indicates, we are at that cliff's edge now.

Figure 2-2. Indiana's age 16-24 population will shrink substantially

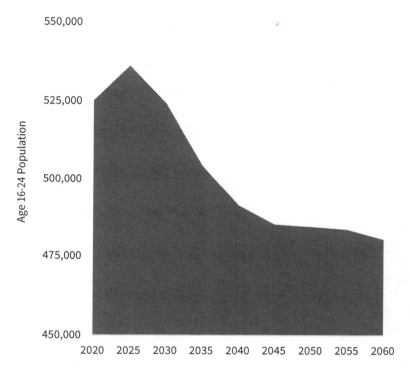

Slowing population growth also translates into ever-smaller gains in the Indiana labor force, especially among those in the prime working and household formation age group of age 25 to 54 due to the losses in the 16 to 24 age population. This projected slow-to-no growth means Indiana will be in a brutal competition to attract working people to the state even as we have improved in business attraction, with dozens of high-dollar investments post-pandemic and the constant drumbeat about struggles to find skilled workers.[1]

Our population among those in prime household formation and working ages is where we will face fierce competition, forcing us to up our game even higher with talent attraction at a time when many other states, facing this same pressure, are upping theirs. Tackling this challenge will take a forward-focused vision combined with ingenuity in policy – all while keeping a keen eye on what our competitors are doing to successfully bring people to their states. The prescription: a combination of quality of life, smart immigration policies and continued investment by the private and public sectors.

PART ONE: THE PEOPLE WE CALL HOOSIERS

To tell this story, we focus on the realities of population and labor force change in the 21st century. Many people remember the economic boom brought about by the baby boom generation. This generation is now in its 60s and 70s and some of its members are still working, but it is not part of that household formation-prime working age that drives economic growth.

What has brought us to this demographic cliff, a phrase originally used by higher education concerning enrollment?[2] Key factors include an ever-shrinking number of births caused by lower fertility rates, an increasing death rate, and the decades-long struggle for Congress to address international migration. Three pictures can quickly tell this story of what drives population growth or decline: births, deaths, and the in-migration of people from other states or countries.

Driver 1: fertility rates and births

An essential facet of household formation, the number of births in Indiana has been on a steep and steady decline since the Great Recession hit in 2008. The 79,000 births in 2023 represent a 12 percent decline compared to 2007. This ranks as the state's third-lowest annual tally since 1946. Only 1987 and 2020 were lower. Meanwhile, the 2022 fertility rate of 59.7 is Indiana's lowest mark on record and almost certainly the lowest in the state's history. To understand how this trend impacts the size and structure of the state's population, Indiana would have had roughly 133,000 more births between 2008 and 2022 if fertility rates from the mid-2000s had remained steady over the past 15 years.

Figure 2-3. Indiana births and fertility rates have dropped

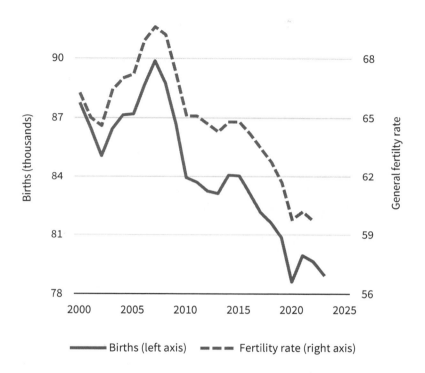

Driver 2: mortality (deaths)

Indiana's life expectancy peaked in 2010 and has since declined, except for a modest post-pandemic rebound. While a variety of factors contribute to Indiana's poor health record, the primary reason for declining life expectancy is a steady rise in mortality rates among the state's working-age population.[3] This will drive Indiana to a decrease in population by 2040 and beyond, which has challenging implications for its future. Figure 2-4 illustrates this shift from more births than deaths ("natural increase") to more deaths than births ("natural decrease"). Note that migration is excluded from natural increase or decrease.

Figure 2-4. Natural increase (decrease) in Indiana population, by decade

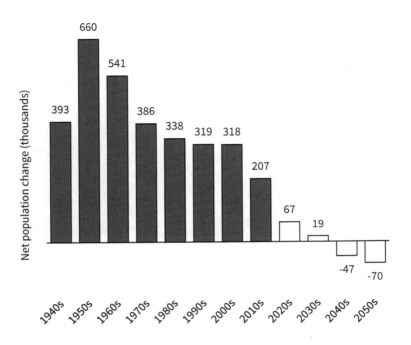

Driver 3: migration

With natural increase expected to fade to natural decrease, migration will become Indiana's sole source of growth. Fortunately, Indiana has proven to be an attractive destination for movers since the 1990s and the state is currently experiencing a surge in migration, with an average annual net inflow of nearly 22,000 residents per year between 2020 and 2023.[4] Given this track record, projections show that Indiana will continue to see a higher level of net in-migration in the 2020s before this measure reverts toward its smaller growth trend in the following decades. Figure 2-5. shows the historical and projected future net migration levels for Indiana from 1940 to 2040.

Figure 2-5. Indiana's net migration by decade, 1940-2050

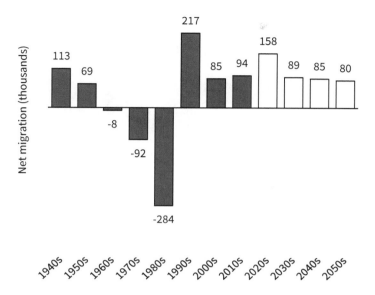

While migration into Indiana is an essential component of change, natural increase has long been Indiana's dominant source of population growth. Even during the 2010s – when net in-migration was relatively robust – natural increase still accounted for 70 percent of Indiana's population growth. However, the natural increase will quickly shift from being a primary driver to a drag on the population.

Magnetic Metros

A handful of metropolitan areas will be responsible for nearly all of Indiana's population growth over the next 30 years. The 11-county Indianapolis metro area will continue to outpace the rest of the state, adding 405,000 residents between 2020 and 2050 – a 19.3 percent increase. The Indy metro area's share of Indiana's total population will rise from 31 percent in 2020 to 35 percent in 2050.

Figure 2-6. Four "Metro Magnets" drive population growth between 2020 and 2040

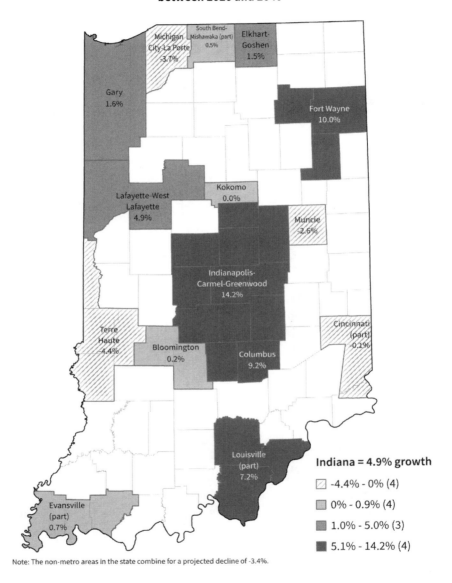

Indiana = 4.9% growth

☐ -4.4% - 0% (4)
☐ 0% - 0.9% (4)
▨ 1.0% - 5.0% (3)
■ 5.1% - 14.2% (4)

Note: The non-metro areas in the state combine for a projected decline of -3.4%.

Figure 2-7. Population growth trajectory reveals stark differences between metro, micropolitan and rural counties

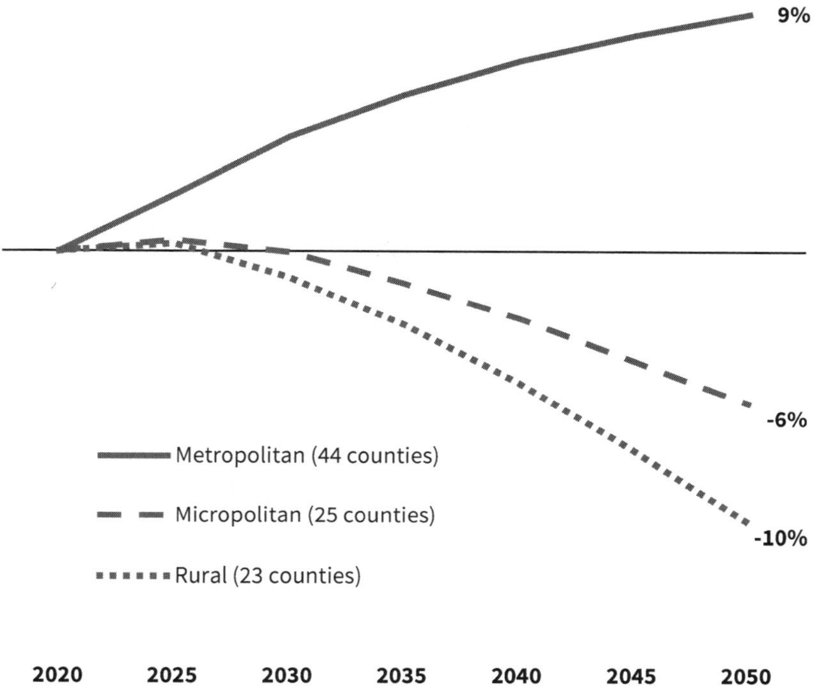

9%

-6%

-10%

━━━━Metropolitan (44 counties)

━ ━ Micropolitan (25 counties)

▪▪▪▪▪▪Rural (23 counties)

2020   2025   2030   2035   2040   2045   2050

What's important to understand is that metropolitan areas are magnets for younger people and will experience the smallest loss of the population younger than age 20 and be the only winner in growth of the age 20 to 64 population (see Figure 2-8). Contrast that with every community gaining in the older than 65 category, and even that age group finds metro areas more appealing.

Why is that? The short answer is that metros have more assets. If we define assets as including housing, schools, colleges, museums and libraries, entertainment, parks, trails and in particular, jobs that turn into careers, then metro areas have all of those assets. Another way to understand the magnetism of metro areas is density – there are more people, there is greater diversity of people across the spectrums of age, origin (be it another state or country), education and interests. There are enough people to offer more choices across industries and lifestyles. And the nature of metro areas is that there are also more choices in terms of population density – not everyone will live in "the big city," but they will be close to it. And that's where the magnetic attraction comes in – drawing people closer to a critical mass of assets. It will be crucial to use and improve those assets to attract people to Indiana. As our birth rate plummets, we depend increasingly, and soon, solely, on migration from other states and countries to Indiana. This remaining source of growth, shown in Figure 2-8, will also mostly concentrate in metro areas.

Figure 2-8. Percent population gains and losses by age group, 2020-2050

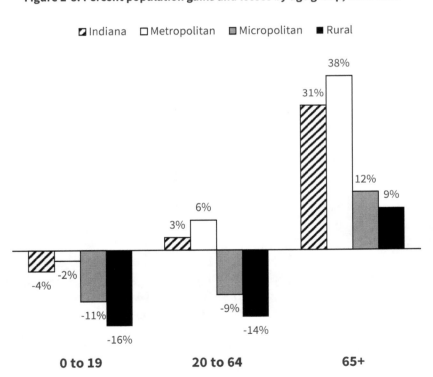

Figure 2-5 (reproduced). Indiana's net migration by decade, 1940-2050.

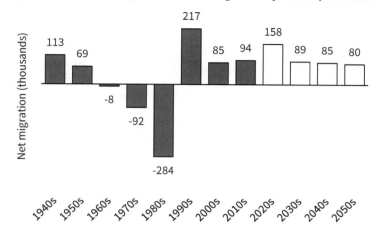

County Gains and Losses

Population losses will hit 67 of Indiana's 92 counties by 2030 and continue, including most of the state's mid-sized and rural communities. Figure 2-9 offers a visual of this forecast. Indiana's rural counties are projected to see a population decline of 10 percent over the next three decades.[5]

Similarly, the state's mid-sized communities – also known as "micropolitan" counties with a city or town that has a population between 10,000 and 50,000 residents – will have a 6 percent drop. Meanwhile, the 44 Indiana counties that are part of a metropolitan statistical area will combine for a 9 percent increase in population over this period.

Hamilton County, the population growth leader in the Indianapolis metro area, will continue to lead the state in growth, with an increase of more than 180,500 residents. During this stretch, Hamilton County will likely overtake Allen County and Lake County and become the state's second most populous county, with a total of approximately 529,500 residents in 2050.

Several other communities in the Indy metro will also continue to see rapid growth. The state's five fastest-growing counties over this projection period will be suburban counties in this region. Boone, Hancock, Hendricks, and Johnson counties will each see their populations grow by at least 25 percent by 2050. Outside central

Indiana, the other communities projected to increase by at least 10 percent over the next three decades are Clark, Warrick, Allen, and Bartholomew counties.

Among Indiana's largest counties, Marion County will add nearly 35,000 residents by 2050 to surpass 1 million people – a 4 percent increase. Allen County will continue its acceleration, climbing by 14 percent over the next 30 years and finishing with a population of nearly 441,000. Lake and St. Joseph counties will see more modest gains through 2035 before beginning to see slight declines, with both counties projected to reach 2050 with fewer residents than they have today.

Figure 2-9. Projected population growth rate by county, 2010-2040, relative to Indiana rate

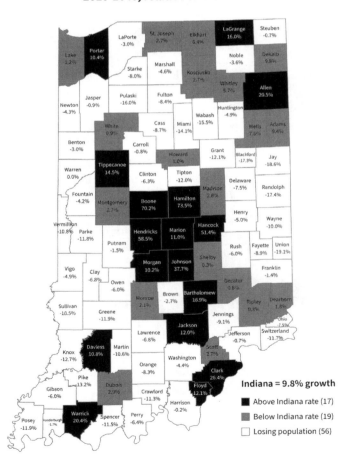

Indiana = 9.8% growth

■ Above Indiana rate (17)
▨ Below Indiana rate (19)
☐ Losing population (56)

Figure 2-10. A majority of 2010-2040 county population change rates are negative

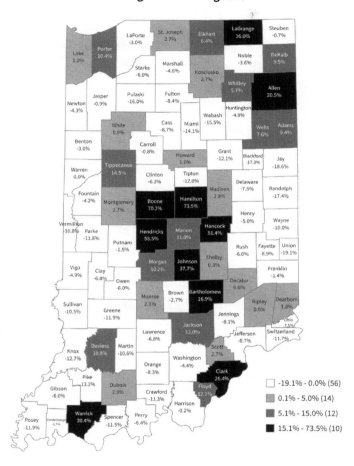

Aging and its Outsized Impact

The aging of the baby boom generation continues to transform our state and the nation inexorably. For instance, in 2010, when the oldest boomers were 64 years old, only 13 percent of Hoosiers were in the 65 and older age group. By 2035, when this entire cohort of boomers will be older than the traditional retirement age, seniors will account for 20 percent of Indiana's population – *from 1 in 10 to 1 in 5 Hoosiers.*

In terms of raw numbers, the size of Indiana's 65 and older age group is projected to grow by nearly 290,000 residents between 2020 and 2035

– a 26 percent increase. The size of the senior population will continue to grow beyond this point and will surpass 1.5 million by 2060 (see Figure 2-11).

Figure 2-11. Indiana population will experience unprecedented changes in its age composition

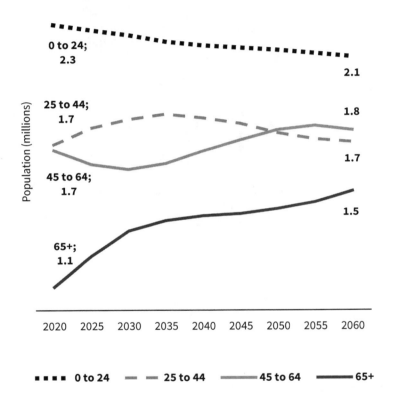

Meanwhile, the size of Indiana's population under the age of 20 is set to fall by 4 percent in the next 30 years. This age group's decline is projected to be particularly sharp in the state's mid-sized and rural counties. Fueled by the state's metro areas, Indiana's working-age population should see modest growth over the next three decades. Of course, this outcome is contingent on net migration to the state remaining strong. Expected declines in this age group for many of the state's mid-sized and rural communities raise concerns about the future size of the labor force in these communities. Examine Figure 2-8 again; what areas have the most growth among young and old?

Figure 2-8 (reproduced). Percent population gains and losses by age group, 2020-2050

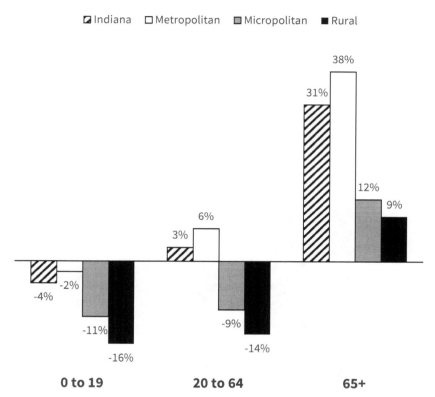

☑ Indiana   ☐ Metropolitan   ▨ Micropolitan   ■ Rural

Perhaps the easiest way to compare aging in counties or states is to look at a single number: median age. In 2020, Indiana's median age of 38.0 was younger than the U.S. mark of 38.5. The median age in Indiana is projected to creep up to 41.3 by 2050. While Indiana is a relatively young state, 61 counties had a median age of 40 or older in 2020. By 2050, 70 Indiana counties will have a median age above 42 years old – see Figure 2-12.

Figure 2-12. Count of Indiana counties by median population age in 2050

Median Age	Number of counties
Over 50	3
45 to 50	30
42 to 44.9	37
40 to 41.9	11
Under 40	11

Other states face similar challenges as Indiana. Figure 2-13 shows Indiana is among 24 states that will grow more slowly than the U.S. average in the decades ahead.

Figure 2-13. Indiana's projected population growth relative to U.S, 2010-2040

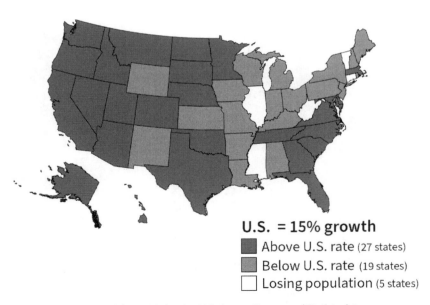

U.S. = 15% growth

Above U.S. rate (27 states)
Below U.S. rate (19 states)
Losing population (5 states)

Source: IBRC (May 2024), using U.S. Census Bureau and Statista data.

PART TWO: THE HOOSIERS WHO WORK

Productivity drives the economy and is generated largely by labor, according to my colleague and economist, Phillip Powell. Indiana needs a labor force right sized in scale (number) and composition (age groups) to meet the needs of business, industry and public service. Despite the opportunities afforded by automation and AI, there are some basic requirements that must be satisfied. Even as we are witnessing the impacts of automation at work, employers are still clamoring for more and higher-skilled labor. As we move into and through this technological revolution, we will continue to see in-demand jobs shift and change, particularly toward the middle-to-higher skill levels. Will Indiana have workers to fill these jobs? Several major indicators are unfavorable.

Slowing labor force growth

The slowing growth of Indiana's population means slow labor force growth. Two charts tell this story over 100 years or more.

Figure 2-14. Indiana's population size by decade 1900 to 2060

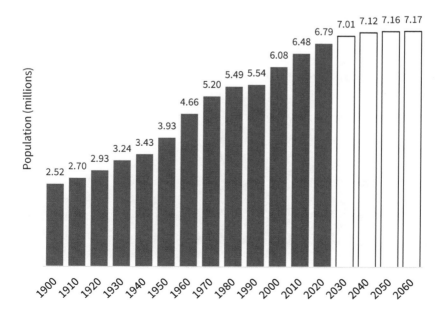

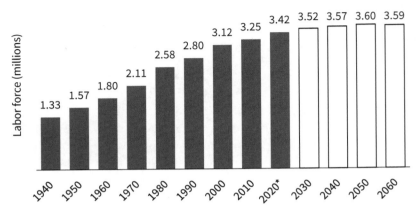

**Figure 2-15. Indiana's labor force size 1940 to 2060
(labor force 16 years of age and older)**

Note: 2020 is an average of 2019 and 2020.

As with our earlier description of Indiana's future population growth, we will show and tell this story visually. Indiana reached 3 million people in the labor force by the 1990s (and 6 million in population). But Indiana has been stuck in the 3 million to 3.5 million range since then. As our population growth has slowed compared to the 20th century, so has the labor growth. The youngest baby boomers will be 66 years old by 2030.

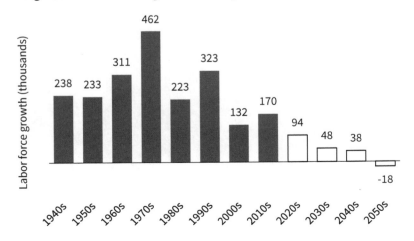

Figure 2-16. Labor force growth slows by 2040s and reverses by 2050s

Notably, female participation rates drove dramatic increases in the labor force between 1950 and 1990. Since then, even as participation between men and women and began to converge, overall participation shrank from nearly 70 percent to closer to 60 percent today. The aging out of the baby boomer generation is partially responsible for this decline, but also sees the reduction in the number of women in the labor force likely caused by the high cost of childcare and the higher cost of living. Such trends raise the question: will we soon see the beginning of the "one car household"?

Figure 2-17. Labor force participation rates, 1940-2060

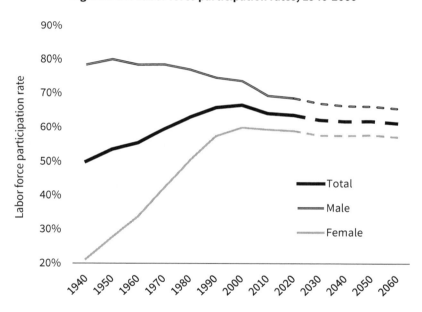

Dearth of prime age workers

While the standard labor force definition since 1950 is those people ages 16 and older, we need to home in on the 25 to 54 age range which drives both household formation and consumption, as well as being in what is called "prime working age." America has long depended on the age 25 to 54 prime working group as the sweet spot for peak consumption of goods and services due to their higher disposable incomes. This is not to say younger or older age groups don't spend money, but they don't do it at the same rate.

So, here is the sobering part of the labor supply story. The age group that feeds into prime working age is shrinking. Here we can see how we move through these age groups. And these trend lines show just how much older our labor force will get by 2040 and beyond.

Figure 2-18. Composite of Indiana labor force size by age groups, 2020-2060

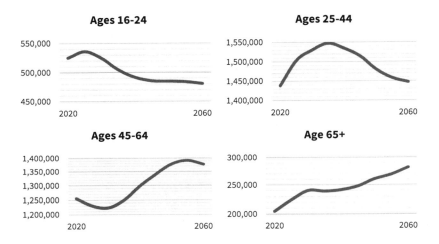

And this is where Indiana will feel the crunch – and the competition – for younger people to live and work here. As noted previously, we will be in a brutal competition for the younger range of workers because our population isn't growing. Across Indiana, we will see metro areas serve as the oasis for labor supply while smaller and more rural areas will be the desert.

Suburban Indianapolis-area counties are expected to have the strongest labor force gains. Similarly, Fort Wayne, New Albany, Evansville, and Columbus can expect double-digit growth over the next 30 years. That leaves 66 of Indiana's 92 counties projected to have a decline in labor force by 2030. This number climbs to 71 by 2050.

Figure 2-19. Labor force gains and losses between 2020 and 2050

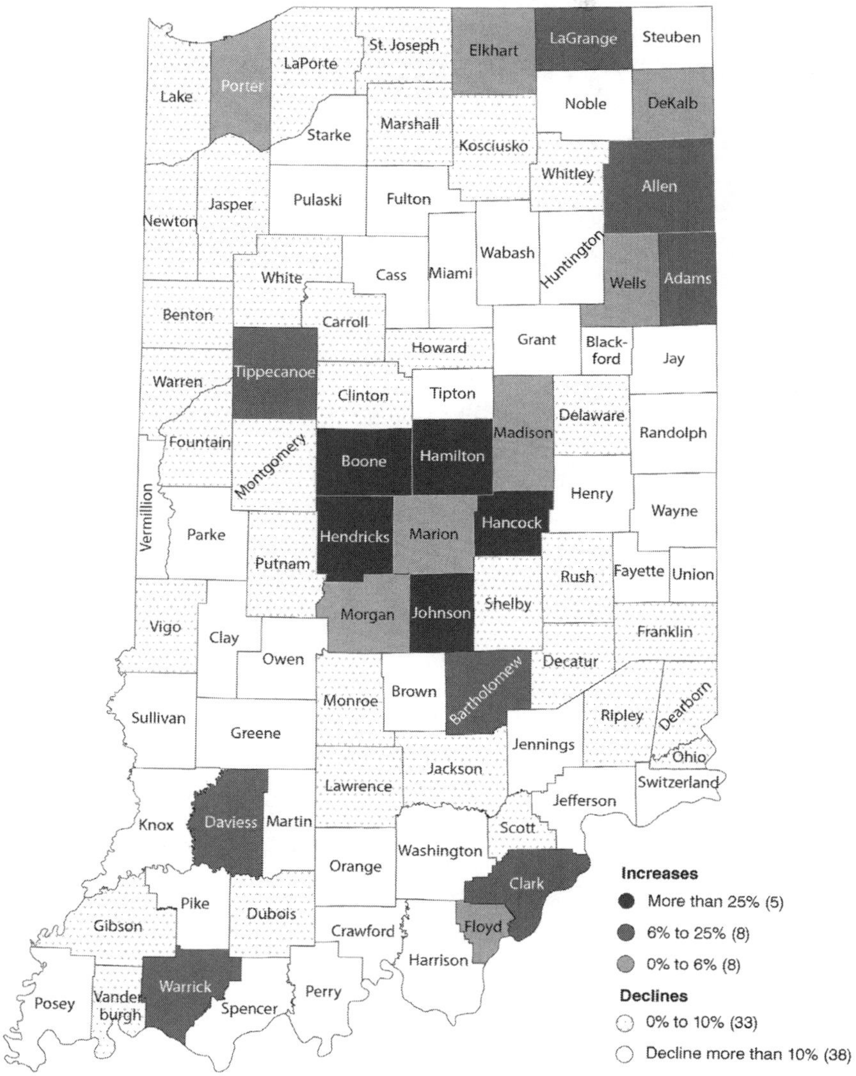

PART THREE: MEETING THE PEOPLE CHALLENGE

Does this forecast seem too stark? Remember that projections are not set in stone; they are predictive, not destiny. The external pressures and economic forces Indiana faces in growing its population and labor supply, along with other states in the Midwest, can be mitigated if not entirely overcome.

1. **From 5 percent to 2 percent: population growth will slow between 2020 and 2040, exacerbated by low fertility rates and higher mortality rates. These trends are very similar to the nation's.**

    Mitigation: A comprehensive evaluation of tax policy that encourages people to stay and move here. We should build on and market our assets better, including geographical location, reasonable cost of living and housing, and quality of life benefits. Access to good schools and the availability of parks, transportation and cultural options matter when prospective residents make location decisions. Public health is our best opportunity to reduce young and middle-aged adult mortality due to drugs and alcohol, smoking, and obesity. Other public policies and programs can be used to enhance cities and towns and provide communities with more tools to make each one uniquely attractive.

2. **States will be in a brutal competition for prime working age adults.**

    Mitigation: Understand what people born in the 21st century want in their community and in their workplace. Population growth in younger people is linked to the availability of assets that are most often associated with metropolitan areas – the magnetic metros concept. Also, take advantage of our proximity to large cities across our borders to build population. For non-metropolitan areas, it will be more important than ever to capitalize on distinguishing assets, especially educational and job opportunities. Furthermore, universal access to broadband is a necessity and not an option for all communities. Indiana will receive more than $868 million in federal internet funding to expand broadband networks, eliminating a barrier for access for many communities and Hoosiers.

3. **Growth will also be affected by immigration, especially from other countries but also from other states. Indiana has continued to show population increases marginally higher than surrounding states but is still losing to the south and west of the nation.**

   Mitigation: Indiana is a net importer of students which is an advantage few states can match. A focus on retaining those graduates can boost population, meet labor supply needs and grow our skilled workforce. Supporting smart immigration strategies is also key to growing Indiana's economy and talent pipeline.

4. **Population growth is tied to the prevalence of innovative and high-growth firms.**

   Mitigation: In addition to the recommendations in Chapter 1, a vital grow factor for these firms is to ensure that the talent pipeline is prepared and available. Chapter 3 provides a framework for combining education reform with innate Hoosier pragmatism and aligning education and career pathways.

CONCLUSION

The future of workforce and demographic trends in Indiana will significantly reshape work and learning in the state. Slowing population growth, an aging workforce, and rapid technological change will increase competition for skilled labor, necessitating greater investments in education, upskilling, and quality of place initiatives to attract people. Employers will need to adapt by fostering continuous learning environments and leveraging technology to enhance productivity. By addressing these challenges proactively, Indiana can create a dynamic and adaptable workforce, ensuring sustained economic growth and innovation. ■

ABOUT INDIANA BUSINESS RESEARCH CENTER

Since 1925, the Indiana Business Research Center (IBRC) has been a leading resource for authoritative analysis and interpretation of economic, demographic, business, housing and education and workforce related issues. The IBRC interprets and provides broad access to the economic and demographic information needed by business, government, education, economic development and nonprofits, as well as individual data users. The Center creates and maintains the large databases needed to support this work and uses its expertise to build user-friendly interactive analytical tools and reports on numerous topics such as income, employment by industry, taxes, education, demographics and a host of other economic indicators for local and regional areas, states and the nation. The IBRC has a long-held reputation for accuracy, objectivity and transparency and is a nationally recognized trustworthy resource.

CHAPTER NOTES

[1] Mark Arend. "Will This Year Beat Last Year's Record Investment?" *Site Selection.* March 2023. https://siteselection.com/issues/2023/ mar/will-this-year-beat-last-years-record-investment.cfm.

[2] Dan Bauman. "Colleges Were Already Bracing for an 'Enrollment Cliff.' Now There Might Be a Second One." *The Chronicle of Higher Education.* February 2024. https://www.chronicle.com/article/colleges-were-already-bracing-for-an-enrollment-cliff-now-there-might-be-a-second-one.

[3] Matt Kinghorn. "Indiana's life expectancy falling further behind U.S." *Indiana Business Review.* Vol 96, No. 2 (Summer 2021). https://www.ibrc.indiana.edu/ibr/2021 /summer/article1.html.

[4] Matt Kinghorn. "Indiana sees stronger population growth in 2023" *Indiana Business Review.* Vol 99, No. 1 (Spring 2024). https://www.ibrc.indiana.edu/ibr/2024/spring/article2.html.

3

The Future of Learning

By Teresa Lubbers and Jacob Baldwin
Sagamore Institute

with contributions from Future of Learning Advisory Group

INTRODUCTION

The future of learning is complex, ever-changing, and increasingly linked to learning opportunities both inside and outside the classroom. As we prepare for changes in the workforce and nature of work, it is essential that we plan for new ways of teaching and learning. Driven by dramatic technological changes that create both uncertainty and opportunity, educators, employers, and policymakers will be challenged to prepare citizens for jobs that don't yet exist and evolving skills needed for personal and economic well-being.

As in past times of economic and workforce revolution, these shifts have the potential to improve personal well-being but also the possibility of leaving people behind and widening income disparity. Creating a culture of continual learning from early childhood to adult reskilling is a requirement – not an option – for a healthy society. The communities that embrace this reality are poised for economic growth and a better future.

In recent years, there has been a blurring of lines between education preparation and workforce needs but not with the sense of urgency that is required. A system based on 20th century ways of learning must be redesigned around 21st century realities, including technological advances and more individualized instruction. Preparing today's learners with work-based learning opportunities is important but again will fall short of meeting individual and employer needs as a new economy emerges. Much of what is learned in both educational and employer settings will become outdated. Hybrid and micro learning will increasingly address the need for reskilling and upskilling. Artificial intelligence will affect nearly every facet and phase of learning.

Metrics of quality, accountability, portability and value must be baked into assessments and system redesign, but what and how they measure progress will change, too. Amid these rapid-fire changes, some elements must be preserved and enhanced, including effective human interaction, critical thinking skills, resiliency, empathy, and equitable opportunity.

Leaders in Indiana must understand the significant trends of innovation and change, adopt a bold and long-term view of what learning in Indiana could be and design a learning system that can grapple with the fast-changing known and not-yet-known implications of the future.

TRENDS IN LEARNING

To effectively prepare for the future, leaders in Indiana must understand the defining trends that will shape how people in Indiana learn. As discussed in the book's introduction, there is an inextricable link between people (workforce), the economy (work), and the ways we are developed and prepared for work and life (learning). This section examines the societal shifts, new technologies and learning options that will affect learners and institutions of learning in the decades to come.

AI will change the role of people in the learning enterprise

As discussed in Chapter 1, artificial intelligence is fundamentally reshaping the "division of labor" between humans and machines in the economy broadly – including learning and education. The boundary lines that define what people and machines do best are changing. We are still testing the frontiers of what AI can do for or with us, and we are determining what limits we will place on AI. Still, we know that the technology's impact on us will be long-term and far-reaching.

The significance and complexity of AI's impact multiplies when we consider that, in addition to altering how we work with computers, AI can imitate us effectively enough that we cannot always identify its presence and use. What we can and need to know is changing, as well as how we know it! These are major shifts that for good reason have animated great enthusiasm and concern from leaders in every corner of society.

Champions of learning and education ought to be especially attuned to these changes in how we produce and distribute knowledge. Jobs will demand varying degrees of literacy with AI. Teachers and learners are using AI and will continue to do so. AI is not just here to stay – it will continue to transform the fabric of society and the learning enterprise.

Technological innovation will create new possibilities for teaching and learning

New possibilities for assessing and personalizing learning are in store for Indiana's learners, too. Augmented and virtual reality (AR/VR) advances will enable us to practice and evaluate complex abilities, like emotional intelligence or soft skills, in immersive simulated environments.[1] Even more information about learners and their learning progress will be digitally recorded as tools make continual assessment easier. Based on these records, AI-enabled tools could be trained to personalize instruction based on each learner's unique profile and point-in-time competency level.

However, the horizon of change will not be limited to "micro-moments" of learning. In higher education, for example, AI will increasingly impact all aspects of the system – including admissions, teaching, assessments, research, student support and operations. Other applications of AI could analyze records of our academic and non-academic learning, our interests, geographic and financial constraints and then recommend the next stage of our learning or jobs where we can apply what we have learned. Learning records and evaluations, even from an early age, could be included in a learner's dataset. Just as manufacturers and pharmaceutical researchers use technology to create digital twins of factories or molecules, the learners of the future will connect to a metaverse, or a virtual reality-based environment that allows users to interact. A learner's AI agent could be instructed to use a digital record of the person's skills and experiences to apply to jobs. An AI agent could also offer coaching to achieve professional goals or even instruct learners in different competencies and knowledge domains.

Experimental technologies like brain-computer interfaces could allow even more information about learners and their learning to be captured and leveraged for personalization.[2] As with any innovation, these technologies hold the promise for tremendous benefit, and for harm and misuse if they are not developed and honed within strong ethical and human-centered design frameworks.

The learners of the future will face even more education and work choices

In the future, Indiana's learners will continue to face a tremendous number of choices of what and how they can learn. Credential Engine, a nonprofit dedicated to mapping learning credentials, identified over 1 million options for U.S. learners, 11,000 of which are offered specifically in Indiana.

Figure 3-1. Learners in the U.S. and Indiana can pursue over a million credential options across four main types of providers.

Credential and provider type	Count of options
Post-secondary institutions - degrees and certificates	350,412
Massive open online courses (MOOC) – completion certificates, micro-credentials and online degrees from foreign universities	13,014
Non-academic providers – badges, course completion certificates, licenses, certifications and apprenticeships	656,505
Secondary schools – diplomas, alternative certificates and high school equivalency diplomas	56,179

Source: Credential Engine (2022).[3]

Numerous forces are converging to create this vast array of choices that learners must find a way to navigate. These forces include the ability for students to quickly travel and relocate to attend schools across the country or to digitally attend schools all over the world; economic specialization that continues to demand workers with unique skillsets; and new technology and tech-enabled industries and occupations that require new competencies.

Furthermore, Indiana students will continue to have an array of schooling options including public schools, public charter schools, private schools, online schools, homeschools, micro-schools and more. The explosion of learning possibilities has ramifications on the entire "learning ecosystem" in Indiana, including student and adult learners, education institutions, businesses, philanthropy and policymakers. Stakeholders in learning will face unique challenges and opportunities from operating in an environment of superabundant and often complex choices.

RECOMMENDATIONS

With these trends in mind, how do we plan for a fast-changing and uncertain future? Our recommendations center on two areas. Indiana must redesign its learning system and improve its navigability.

Indiana should (re)design its learning system

Learning in Indiana needs to change. Today, learning is supported by an architecture that is not designed for the present or prepared for the future. Our individual and economic needs are profoundly different than the past and will continue to evolve. The five recommendations that follow offer leaders of learning a framework and principles that can help usher in a new era of growth and prosperity.

The experts we interviewed to help inform this chapter also wrestled to define how systematic Indiana's learning system truly is across our people's lifetime learning journey. Parts of our learning and education system are coordinated and other parts operate as silos and with less collective purpose. A major and foundational aspect of our recommendations is that Indiana develops the capacity to redesign its learning system through an effort to bring all the stakeholders to the table and forge a consensus about greater cooperation and shared mission in future-informed service of learners in Indiana. The Governor's Workforce Cabinet should be better leveraged to partner with employers to develop and operationalize a shared vision.

1. Cultivate lifelong learning and learning agility skills

A commitment to lifelong learning recognizes that Indiana's people are our greatest natural resource and asset. We need to offer experiences that develop Hoosiers at all stages of life. This includes quality early childhood programs for Hoosiers aged 0-3 when much of the brain's architecture for the rest of life is formed. Our pre-kindergarten through 12th-grade education providers are uniquely positioned to provide opportunities for career exploration and to develop character qualities that will enable adaptation in the face of change. Lifelong learning also means providing options for adults who want to pursue jobs in new fields or industries and need opportunities to develop their skills.

Given the technological and economic shifts already underway, the learning system must also cultivate life-long "learning agility," or "the ability to remain open to new ways of thinking and to continuously learn new skills."[4] Current and future generations will need the ability to adapt and respond to changes with agency and resilience; our learning system must explicitly name this goal and offer opportunities for learners to practice and acquire these skills.

Finally, as we continue to build the talent pipeline needed for economic development we must also hold on to the importance of learning and education's role in personal, family and community development. Our state will be the healthiest when our learning system balances economic advancement with strong neighborhood, social and civic ties. A lifelong learning system will cultivate these values and skills and will be best realized by the joint support of families, schools and employers.

2. Ensure students are prepared for good jobs in the future economy

Indiana's learning system should also include, especially for the next generation, a commitment to develop a core set of skills in each student that will prepare them for gainful employment in the economy of the future. As Brookings Institute highlighted in 2021, nearly half of Indiana's jobs in some regions of the state neither offer a living wage nor a pathway to a living wage![5] The learning system must do its part both to prepare students for gainful employment in jobs and skillsets that will evolve in the coming years. Much of the current public discourse about the value of a college degree and the demand for greater alignment between learning and work stems from this reasonable desire. It is important to note that higher education institutions are adapting to this expectation by building career awareness and preparation into their degrees and programs. Holistic, lifelong human development across education providers must be balanced with and include strategic, future-informed preparation for good jobs.

As discussed in Chapter 8, employers have a responsibility and an economic incentive to invest more in talent development. Employers are uniquely able to offer learning institutions in Indiana feedback about the types of skillsets and workers they will need 10 and 20 years from now. This feedback can be synthesized into a core set of skills and traits that educators can incorporate into a broader vision for human development. Policymakers can incentivize or compensate enterprises to engage in this work, especially small and medium-sized enterprises with less discretionary resources. Philanthropic or community organizations can offer space for cross-sector leaders to convene and align in effective collaborations and information exchanges that meet employer, community and individual needs. Indiana has multiple examples of communities and regions that have built prosperity through these types of cross-sector partnerships.

A sustainably prosperous future for Indiana can come about only if our learning system is designed to prepare people for gainful employment in the economy of today and tomorrow.

3. Better connect our talent to the economy through reimagined credentialing

In addition to our formal learning environment and assessments, Indiana should invent and adopt new ways to measure the outcome of learning – competencies. Traditional credentials like diplomas and degrees capture a partial picture of an individual's ability to contribute and often require a large time or financial commitment to an academic institution. Many capable individuals in Indiana have high potential to contribute to the economy but are not able to obtain the credentials they need. As competition intensifies for prime age workers in the decades ahead, Indiana can both attract and retain talent if its credential providers can nimbly and affordably credential learners' competencies.

Indiana should lean into disruptive technologies and credentialing models to spur local innovation and emulate pilots in other states. Employers are willing to experiment; many have dropped college degree requirements for certain positions. Now, we need credentialing pioneers and technical experts who can invent and operationalize ways of evaluating the quality of learners' competencies rather than where they were acquired.

As our learning and employment systems grow in their ability to recognize these and other forms of "out of school" learning, those systems can better guide people's development and employment opportunities. Innovations in credentialing can start in high-demand jobs of the future that offer gainful employment. Indiana can become a magnet for talented individuals excluded by outdated credentialing systems elsewhere.

4. Embrace technologies and shape them to the advantage of human learning

Many well-intentioned leaders have pointed to the dangers of new technologies, especially as we have begun to better understand their negative effects. Social media and smartphones, for example, have rightly been questioned for their effect on childhood development and mental health. However, short of a new Dark Age, it is difficult to "undiscover" a technological breakthrough. Technologies themselves are usually not good or bad; how people use a technology determines its effect. Any productivity gains AI offers teachers in Indiana could help alleviate our teacher shortage, for example. Therefore, we must engage and actively shape new technologies to advantage human learning and flourishing.

The president of the Lumina Foundation, an Indianapolis-based private foundation dedicated to expanding post-secondary learning, penned an article for *Forbes* last year that offers insightful counsel about what form of engagement can best shape AI.

"For artificial intelligence, we need more than just a legal framework; we need an individual rights and responsibilities framework. That ethical frame should include our approach to higher education, one that both engages with AI's ethical implications, and helps prepare people for the work that only humans can do." [6]

– Jamie Merisotis
President, Lumina Foundation

Part of embracing new technology is also questioning established norms and approaches. For AI, this means recognizing and creating widespread awareness of how it has changed the "division of labor" between people and the advanced algorithms that power AI. We must prepare students especially *to use rather than compete with AI*.[7] Students should become AI natives because that technology will become as foundational to the future Indiana as writing or using computers is for us today. By engaging AI and other new technologies, we can learn and spread their best uses and arrest harmful applications. If we give up our seat at the table by resisting change, then these technologies will be developed without us and could evolve in damaging ways.

Finally, we must seek balance in our development of technology. Yes, we should leverage new technology to its fullest extent to more personally serve learners – identifying high-value learning topics faster, empowering teachers with better tools, and analyzing data to identify the best learning approaches for each student. However, we must still endow students with a shared set of beliefs, experiences, and values that enable them to understand each other and engage respectfully in the marketplace and community. We should not make learning so individualized and digitized that people become isolated and disconnected from each other, the needs of their community and their shared humanity.

5. Ensure quality and value through data, governance and measurement

Finally, the learning system must ensure quality and value for learners. Shared governance with oversight and multiple checks and balances can ensure that no single stakeholder's needs dominate. Integrated data systems can ensure portability and interoperability among all parts of the learning system. Also, new ways to measure proficiency, quality, and value will be key so that there is a clear picture of learning strengths and opportunities for all members of the learning system. If competencies become a standard for preparation and knowledge, the shared system of measurement must be regularly updated and ensure readiness and opportunity. As choices and options proliferate, the value and importance of a set of effective standards to ensure quality and value is more difficult and more needed.

Indiana's learning ecosystem needs new navigation resources and tools

Future-minded leaders should also prioritize making Indiana's learning systems highly navigable for individuals and organizations. In a world of rapid change and dizzying options, additional support and structure is essential to preserve learners' sense of agency and personal effectiveness. The following recommendations suggest approaches to remove barriers for individuals and organizations, so they function better.

1. Build strong intermediary organizations to simplify complexity

Intermediary organizations can contribute a powerful role that enhances the learning and workforce development landscape in Indiana. In a world with millions of workers, learning pathways and employers, coordinating intermediaries can facilitate connections and reduce crippling complexity for all stakeholders. Examples of the value proposition of intermediaries abound. For example, many companies want to hire qualified high school graduates, but firms become overwhelmed when multiple high schools contact them. High schools face the similar problem of finding the right employer connections in a sea of options. An intermediary that specializes in maintaining relationships with the all the stakeholders in a region can facilitate connections among them and improve the discovery process for learners, jobseekers and employers.

Intermediaries can also contribute a vital role to industries with anemic or non-existent talent and talent development pathways. While individual companies – and especially small and medium-sized companies that employ many Hoosiers – may not have the margin to build intermediary infrastructure, a group of companies that pool their resources can. Just as some industry intermediaries lobby for legislative change, other intermediaries can secure an industry's future through talent pipelines and development pathways. Cost-saving economies of scale occur when some talent and development infrastructure is shared instead of being fully replicated at each firm. Especially in Indiana industries where the average employee age creeps higher and higher, companies face an imperative to ensure their survival and growth.

Finally, relatively more initiatives and programs exist that offer learners and opportunity seekers an entry point to a new profession.

Often less thought is given to a person's second, third, and fourth roles. There must be a ladder of opportunity that allows for continued growth and development within an occupation or industry. Read more about the important role of employers as educators in Chapter 8.

For insight into a recent example of the powerful value proposition of intermediaries, read the case study by the Central Indiana Corporate Partnership (CICP) on workforce intermediaries in Indiana at the end of this chapter.

2. Offer learners and opportunity seekers in Indiana better decision-making tools and resources

Technologies can significantly enhance some parts of searching for learning or employment opportunities.

AI-driven matching tools can scan and analyze vast amounts of data from job postings, candidate profiles, and educational programs. These tools can provide personalized matches, helping learners find suitable jobs and businesses find the right talent quickly and efficiently.

Digital achievement wallets can store and verify learners' credentials, skills, and accomplishments in a secure, easily accessible format. This technology can offer smoother transitions between educational institutions and employers, ensuring that learners' achievements are recognized throughout their career journeys.

Learners would also benefit from access to a collection of resources that provide continually updated information about educational programs, job pathways and competency requirements in Indiana specifically. These "meta-level" resources can guide learners through the complex landscape of lifelong learning and career development.

As they make learning and employment decisions, learners in Indiana and their families need an authoritative guide to the in-demand skills of the future economy that is widely available and regularly updated with employer input. Indiana leaders can clarify long-term pathways to prosperity through this high standard for resources intended to guide learners in Indiana.

These tools must be accompanied with marketing and publicity initiatives that will reach young people and adults and offer information in an accessible and relevant way.

3. Leave no learners behind

Indiana's changing demographics highlight the urgency of addressing the needs of learners being left behind. Large numbers of Black, Hispanic, low-income, rural, male and adult learners are at risk of being left behind in the new economy. At a time when the population is becoming more diverse, bold reforms will be essential to ensure that all learners, especially those facing multiple barriers, are prepared for the jobs of the future. The future learning environment will have abundant choices, and to remain competitive and prosperous Indiana must create pathways for all learners.

AI and technological change could exacerbate these achievement and socioeconomic disparities in Indiana, if not developed carefully. A 2023 Pew Research Center survey found that "about half of upper-income Americans had high awareness of AI (52 percent), compared with just 15 percent of lower-income adults."[8]

Widespread internet broadband access will become even more important as AI increases the importance and centrality of computers in our society. However, AI also holds the promise of better support for learners; as teachers are freed from some of the routine parts of their job, they will have more time to focus on engaging students and meeting individual needs.[9]

Indiana must support learners who are struggling or cannot access the learning system, so that we do not miss out on their potential and contribution. Our prosperity depends on all Hoosiers participating. We cannot afford or accept a future where some of our neighbors are left behind.

CONCLUSION

Indiana is fortunate in the number of assets that leaders can leverage to build the future of learning for the people and jobs of 2040. Pioneers in the private, public, and philanthropic sectors are driving innovation through thoughtful risk-taking and prescient preparation with a long-term mindset.

The redesign of high school, properly developed and implemented, has the potential to empower learners and local leaders to customize learning for their context and opportunities. Indiana is already a net importer of learners who travel from all over the country and world to attend our public and private institutions. The leaders of our business and learning communities are service-minded and unusually willing to collaborate on practical solutions for challenges facing our state. Our state also has a well-endowed philanthropic sector that supports a laboratory of learning that identifies and scales the strongest strategies and solutions for Indiana learners.

However, these assets are valuable only to the extent that they are mobilized by leaders who seek the good of all in Indiana through a bold vision for change and reform. Our challenges are great and, in many households, Hoosiers are already experiencing a foretaste of an unequal and deteriorating future.

Take a moment to consider your vision for the future of learning in Indiana. Why do people go to school and what do they need to know before they leave? How do we support them when they need to return to gain new skills? How do we balance the possibilities of what technological advances can do while determining what limits are appropriate? What do we measure and value in a newly designed learning system? The future we imagine for ourselves has significant – perhaps the greatest – bearing on what we will create by 2040.

In writing this chapter, the authors sought counsel from leaders of learning institutions in Indiana that serve people of all ages, from infants to our most experienced adults. We asked these learning experts and advocates, many of whom have given decades of service to helping Hoosiers learn, what they thought a bright future of learning for Indiana looks like.

With surprising agreement, they voiced that the best of Indiana could be brought out in a future where Hoosiers keep learning throughout their lives, where learning balances personalization with shared values, and learning integrates with work to provide individual flourishing. Above all, these leaders stressed that Indiana's greatest assets are its people, and that is the lens through which we must consider how we plan future systems, policies, and investments and cultivate skills, knowledge, and character.

We challenge you to imagine and prepare for not just the problems of today, but tomorrow as well and to invite others along with you as we build the future of learning in Indiana together. ■

CHAPTER 3 CASE STUDY

The Importance of Workforce Intermediaries to a Robust Economy

By Melina Kennedy
The Central Indiana Corporate Partnership

Prosperity requires a dynamic economy. One in which companies are constantly evolving to derive greater and greater value from the goods and services they offer to customers and clients. And, of course, companies require access to workers with skills needed to enable all of this. However, as has been evident in recent years, it's not always easy for companies to find workers. There is frequent misalignment between the skills employers need and the skills prospective employees offer. This is why intermediaries can be an essential link in creating critical connections and developing solutions. The workforce is one area where the value of intermediaries is especially pronounced because they can mitigate the mismatch between the supply and demand for workers.

Role of workforce intermediaries

Often, workforce intermediaries are non-profit organizations with a focus on a particular industry cluster or population of the workforce. One might first ask what is a workforce intermediary? The answer may be subjective but at least one source, the Urban Institute, defines workforce intermediaries and collaboratives as "organizations that bring together partners in the workforce system to identify workforce needs; plan, develop, and implement strategies; and raise funds to support these strategies."[10] Some may challenge the appropriateness of the term "intermediary" as not being descriptive enough of the power and impact that intermediaries can play in defining and implementing game changing solutions, as was the case in a recent meeting that I joined of six other peer regions where this topic was discussed. I think there is probably a better term than intermediary, but regardless of the right name, the concept is what matters.

By collaboratively bringing together individual external partners to build a more cohesive ecosystem, intermediaries can conquer silos that act as barriers to a coordinated and most effective system. When it comes to a well-operated workforce ecosystem, effective intermediaries tackle workforce challenges by addressing the needs of both employers and potential employees, ideally well ahead of the actual need. They bring together stakeholders to identify workforce needs, leveraging important work such as the important findings thoughtfully laid out in this book, and rally together to develop and implement strategies needed to plan proactively and respond.

When done right, workforce intermediaries can help guide investment and action by the broader community to make a real impact by bringing the right partners together to identify in advance and ultimately translate the future talent needs of employers into strategic, actionable strategies. And by bringing together organizations to set common vision and goals and then lead the necessary coordinated assessment of capabilities, assets and gaps to set a strategic view and action plan, they can catalyze and organize the rally cry around what needs to happen to ensure outcomes that meet that common vision and goals and lead to broader economic prosperity.

Intermediaries accelerate apprenticeship innovation in Indiana

Indiana is fortunate to have a number of intermediaries that play a role in creating a sustained, prosperous economy. The Central Indiana Corporate Partnership (CICP) brings together chief executive officers of some of our most prominent companies, universities and philanthropy to focus on our advanced industries. CICP largely operates through four branded sector initiatives focusing on the life sciences, agbiosciences, advanced manufacturing and tech industries.

In addition to the industry-specific initiatives, CICP formed Ascend Indiana in 2016 to serve as a workforce intermediary to bring together employers, education providers, and other key partners in the workforce ecosystem to foster alignment among Indiana's advanced industries, educational institutions that supply their talent, and the nonprofit, philanthropic, and governmental stakeholders positioned to influence the relevant talent pipelines.

Indiana's youth apprenticeship programs, which are currently operating across five community-based pilot programs, are based on the successful apprenticeship model in Switzerland. Ascend Indiana played a role in this work as a workforce intermediary by partnering with communities to launch their pilot programs by supporting program design and delivering technical assistance. Additionally, Ascend launched a statewide Community of Practice that convenes more than

100 education, industry, and government leaders to learn from the successes and challenges of the pilot programs with the goal of systems-level change and growing youth apprenticeship at scale in Indiana.

Conclusion

Many partners came together to play different roles in this work including workforce investments boards, secondary and post-secondary schools, employers, funders and others who could benefit from the expert guidance, consistency and structure offered by the pilot work and Community of Practice. As this model grows in scale, workforce intermediaries like Ascend Indiana, and other industry-led intermediaries will be even more important to accomplish this work by proactively identifying the most-needed jobs by key industry sectors, most-needed skills and attributes for those jobs, and even curriculum development. This is just one example of the kind of role that workforce intermediaries can play in ensuring that a wide variety of stakeholders come together to identify needs in advance, plan strategies, and work to execute a plan.

Indiana has a long history of people and organizations working collaboratively, across party lines, to get great things done. The role that intermediaries will play to ensure that this collective forethought is leveraged and used to guide our work ahead is both exciting and essential. ■

ABOUT SAGAMORE INSTITUTE

Sagamore Institute was founded in 2004 as a heartland-based, action-oriented think tank. We operate a network of scholars, policy experts and innovators to advance solutions to the world's biggest problems. Our ideas travel in two directions: we move upstream to change policy and reform systems, and we travel downstream to put ideas to work via best practices to improve lives and the places we live. Sagamore's three pillars of action are focused on creating opportunity, ensuring national security and advancing civil society. For this chapter, Sagamore received valuable counsel from an advisory group consisting of: Jay Akridge, Jason Bearce, Scott Bess, Stephanie Bothun, Brandon Brown, Molly Dodge, David Hummels, Kermit Kaleba, Dottie King, Marie Mackintosh, PJ McGrew, David Shane and Maureen Weber.

ABOUT CENTRAL INDIANA CORPORATE PARTNERSHIP

The Central Indiana Corporate Partnership (CICP) was formed in 1999 to bring together the chief executives of the region's prominent corporations, foundations and universities in a strategic and collaborative effort dedicated to Indiana's continued prosperity and growth. To advance this mission, CICP sponsors five key talent and industry sector initiatives, AgriNovus Indiana, Ascend Indiana, BioCrossroads, Conexus Indiana and TechPoint, each of which addresses challenges and opportunities unique to its respective area: agbiosciences, talent and workforce development, life sciences, advanced manufacturing and logistics, and technology. To learn more about CICP, visit www.cicpindiana.com.

CHAPTER NOTES

[1] For two early-stage examples of this type of application for VR/AR, consider the Project Overcome initiative sponsored by Goodwill Industries International and Accenture or the immersive learning company Talespin by Cornerstone.

[2] Yifan Wang, Shen Hong, and Crystal Tai. "China's Efforts to Lead the Way in AI Start in Its Classrooms." *Wall Street Journal.* October 24, 2019. https://www.wsj.com /articles/chinas-efforts-to-lead-the-way-in-ai-start-in-its-classrooms-11571958181.

CHAPTER NOTES (cont.)

[3] Credential Engine. *Counting U.S. Postsecondary and Secondary Credentials.* Washington, DC: Credential Engine. 2002. https://credentialengine.org/wp-content/uploads/2023/01/Final-CountingCredentials_2022.pdf.

[4] Adam Mitchinson and Robert Morris. *Learning About Learning Agility.* Center for Creative Leadership. 2014. https://cclinnovation.org/wp-content/uploads/2020/02/learningagility.pdf.

[5] Mark Muro, Robert Maxim, and Jacob Whiton. *State of Renewal: Charting a new course for Indiana's economic growth and inclusion.* Brookings Institution. February 2021. https://www.brookings.edu/articles/state-of-renewal-charting-a-new-course-for-indianas-economic-growth-and-inclusion.

[6] Jamie Merisotis. "AI Systems Need A Conscience—And That's Us." *Forbes.* November 29, 2023. https://www.forbes.com/sites/jamiemerisotis/2023/11/29/ai-systems-need-a-conscience-and-thats-us.

[7] Jill Anderson interview with Chris Dede. "Educating in a World of Artificial Intelligence." Harvard Graduate School of Education. February 9, 2023. https://www.gse.harvard.edu/ideas/edcast/23/02/educating-world-artificial-intelligence.

[8] Brian Kennedy, Alec Tyson and Emily Saks. "Public Awareness of Artificial Intelligence in Everyday Activities." Pew Research Center. February 15, 2023. https://www.pewresearch.org/science/2023/02/15/public-awareness-of-artificial-intelligence-in-everyday-activities.

[9] Jill Anderson interview with Chris Dede. "Educating in a World of Artificial Intelligence."

[10] "Workforce Intermediaries and Collaboratives." Urban Institute Local Workforce System Guide. 2022. https://workforce.urban.org/taxonomy/term/30.html.

4

The Manufacturing Renaissance

By Fred Cartwright
Conexus Indiana

with contributions from
Butler University, the Indiana Manufacturers Association, Ivy Tech
Community College and Purdue University

INDIANA'S PIVOTAL ROLE IN THE MANUFACTURING RENAISSANCE

Today, advanced manufacturing is responsible for nearly 30 percent of our state's Gross Regional Product and nearly 20 percent of the workforce, making it Indiana's largest and most intensive industry sector. The statistics paint the same picture: the prosperity of Hoosiers, their families and our state's communities depend on the health and resilience of the advanced manufacturing base.

Making products – from automobiles to life-saving medicines, electronics to medical devices – is the socioeconomic backbone of Indiana's economy, providing not just good wages and benefits, but a sense of identity to the more than 700,000 Hoosiers who create and deliver the products needed and used around the world every day.

Nationally, the manufacturing sector renders a similar story. It accounts for roughly $2.4 trillion in GDP, employing more than 12 million people.[1] And according to McKinsey & Company, while the industry represents only about 11 percent to 15 percent of U.S. GDP, the "sector makes an extensive economic contribution, including 20 percent of the nation's capital investment, 35 percent of productivity growth, 60 percent of exports and 70 percent of business R&D spending."[2]

Yet, the United States as a whole is poised to capitalize on what could be called a "manufacturing renaissance" fueled by recent policy developments at the federal level and a shift toward onshoring production of critical products.

Onshoring production of critical products

After a long period of globalization that saw many critical raw materials and components outsourced to overseas facilities, such as components for health-care products and electronics, companies are beginning to rethink their supply chain strategies. Cost reduction has been a primary driver for manufacturers to maintain an international footprint, but shifting global demographics and ongoing supply chain disruptions are changing the cost-benefit equation. These factors will make onshoring more attractive for companies in the future.

America's infrastructure readiness will enable or hinder industrial growth

Industrial economies rely heavily on robust infrastructure, including reliable and affordable energy, water, roads and railways, airports as well as telecommunications (i.e., 5G and broadband). During the first and second industrial revolutions (Industry 1.0 and 2.0), the U.S. was a top performer in infrastructure investment and development. However, substantial concerns have been raised due to America's aging infrastructure and lack of investment in recent years.[3]

The energy grid is one example that is critical to the success of our manufacturing sector. Energy has been relatively cheap and reliable in the U.S. compared to other regions, but energy costs have been steadily increasing, particularly post-pandemic.[4] In addition to rising costs, America's electric grid is undergoing a transition period to include new sources of clean energy. Indiana also continues to add more renewable power sources, such as wind and solar, to its energy mix.[5]

Should the manufacturing renaissance take hold in Indiana and the nation, energy demand could eclipse energy supply without significant grid enhancements from the public and private sectors.[6] The speed and scale at which grid infrastructure can be upgraded or transitioned could be a limiting factor for industry growth, and by extension, affect future workforce demand.

On the other hand, new bills such as the Infrastructure Investment and Jobs Act, could turn the tide for America's infrastructure readiness and its ability to support new growth across the industrial economy. For now, the outlook is presumed favorable in some camps, but in others, America's infrastructure readiness is yet to be seen.

Federal manufacturing policy tailwinds

With significant legislation signed into law, such as the Inflation Reduction Act (IRA) and CHIPS and Science Act, new incentives and funding are available for private sector investments and manufacturing facility construction. According to the U.S. Treasury, construction spending for manufacturing hit $200 billion, more than doubling since 2021 (Figure 4-1), with a significant portion of these dollars (about 50 percent) supporting investments in semiconductors and microelectronics. [7]

Figure 4-1. Real total manufacturing construction spending, 2005-2024

Source: Nostrand, U.S. Dept. of Treasury (July 2024). [8]

Notes: Value of Private Construction Put in Place for Manufacturing, U.S. Census Bureau. Monthly at a seasonally adjusted, annualized rate. Nominal spending delated by the producer Price Index for Intermediate Demand Materials and Components for Construction, Bureau of Labor Statistics.

Moreover, a White House investment tracker, which includes both public and private sector investments, shows $395 billion invested in semiconductors and microelectronics and another $173 billion for electric vehicles (EVs) and batteries, $77 billion for clean energy manufacturing and infrastructure and $28 billion for biomanufacturing. [9]

Indiana has also enjoyed success of its own. Three notable examples are SK hynix Inc.'s plan to invest close to $4 billion to build an advanced packaging fabrication and R&D facility for artificial intelligence (AI) products in the Purdue Research Park; a $2.5 billion investment by Stellantis and Samsung SDI Co. to build a next-generation battery plant in Kokomo, as the auto industry ramps up production of electric vehicles; and a $9 billion investment by Eli Lilly in the LEAP District to produce the ingredients for its weight loss drugs.[10,11]

The manufacturing renaissance has already begun in the U.S. and in Indiana. All eyes should be locked on how Indiana's manufacturing sector responds to these new opportunities and challenges.

A global leadership position in manufacturing is earned, not given.

What we do collectively in the next two decades will undoubtedly have lasting implications upon Indiana's economic competitiveness for years to come. Prosperity through 2040 will require collective action and new pathways to overcome monumental disruptors knocking at our door: including a technological revolution and rapidly changing labor market.

CHALLENGES FOR PROSPERITY BY 2040

An increasingly high-tech and digital manufacturing sector will widen an already pressing skills gap

With the onset of the Fourth Industrial Revolution (better known as Industry 4.0 or Smart Manufacturing), Indiana's manufacturing sector is experiencing a widening skills gap, particularly within small- to mid-sized firms. In fact, according to Deloitte, an estimated 3.8 million jobs will be created in the coming years and 1.9 million manufacturing positions could remain unfilled in the United States through 2033 due to the industry's growing skills shortage (Figure 4-2).[12]

Figure 4-2. Projection of unfilled manufacturing jobs from 2024 to 2033

Sources of U.S. manufacturing job openings from 2024 to 2033

Jobs from IIJA, IRA, and CHIPS and Science Act	6%	0.2 million
Open jobs from industry growth	20%	0.8 million
Jobs from retirements	74%	2.8 million
TOTAL		3.8 million

Projection of skills shortage shortfall in manufacturing

Vacant positions due to skills shortage	50%	1.9 million
Jobs likely to be filled	50%	1.9 million
TOTAL		3.8 million

Data source: Deloitte analysis of U.S. Bureau of Labor Statistics and Invest.gov data[13]

Adoption of digital technologies, which are necessary to increase productivity and remain competitive in a global environment, will further accentuate this skills gap. Advanced technologies and digital tools come with increased requirements for an educated, tech-savvy workforce that is prepared to not just work alongside these technologies but consistently navigate and manage change. In 2018, McKinsey & Company estimated a whopping 14 percent decrease in hours worked on physical and manual skills and a 55 percent increase in hours worked on technical skills by 2030.[14] If revised in today's numbers, this estimation would likely be even more pronounced.

A constrained labor market will see fewer workers available to a growing sector

Indiana may face unprecedented labor market challenges in the coming years, according to local and national economists. Stagnating population growth, declining labor force and labor force participation rate, and baby boomer retirements will affect our workforce availability (Figure 4-3 and Figure 4-4).[15] While automation, digital adoption and a global landscape may lead to an overall decrease in total factory jobs, if the status quo continues, Indiana's labor market could be the limiting factor on industry growth.

Furthermore, according to national technology-based economic development firm TEConomy Partners, "workforce availability and skills represent crucial concerns for Indiana and are the primary rate-limiting factor for economic growth."[16] The challenge spans multiple facets, too, including our "K-12 education performance, the percentage of the population seeking higher education credentials, and the retention and attraction of personnel with in-demand educational credentials and occupational skills."[17] Simply put, manufacturers will not have the "typical pathway" of putting more people to work to grow their companies and their output.

Figure 4-3. Indiana labor force projections through 2060

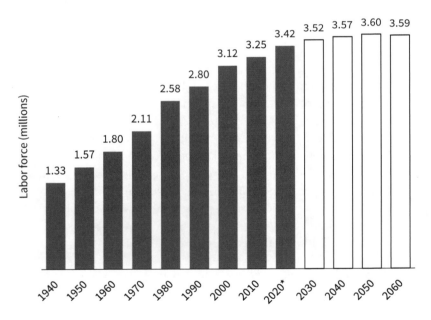

Source: Indiana Business Research Center (2024).[18]

*Note: 2020 is an average of 2019 and 2020; labor force of persons 16 years of age and older

Figure 4-4. Labor force participation rates through 2060

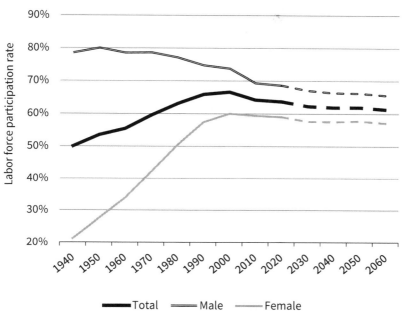

Source: Indiana Business Research Center (2024).[19]

Indiana's manufacturing sector must undergo a cultural transformation to align with the future workforce

By 2040, a majority of the baby boomer workforce will have reached the expected retirement age, and millennials, Gen Z and Gen Alpha Hoosiers will account for a significant portion of the available workforce (Figure 4-5).[20] Values alignment between Gens Z and Alpha and the manufacturing sector is particularly a cause for concern. According to a 2024 McKinsey & Company study that explored Gen Z's relationship with employment in manufacturing, "Gen Z workers say they're open to jobs in manufacturing, but getting them to take these jobs, engage and stay will mean changing a work environment long optimized for machines, not people."[21]

To attract and retain these natively tech-savvy workers, the manufacturing sector will need to consider adjusting what might be called a "rigid culture." Traditionally, manufacturing production has been human powered through manual tasks that require people to be present in a certain place at a certain time. But automation and technology adoption will afford companies more flexibility as workers are less tied to specific workstations and more focused on the supervision of automated processes. This new level of flexibility can be leveraged to entice the next generation of workers into open positions and allow firms to make systemic changes to their culture.

Figure 4-5. Projected Indiana labor force size by age through 2050 (millions)

Labor Force Age Group	2020	2025	2030	2035	2040	2045	2050
16 to 24	0.53	0.54	0.52	0.50	0.49	0.49	0.48
25 to 44	1.44	1.50	1.53	1.55	1.53	1.51	1.48
45 to 64	1.26	1.23	1.22	1.25	1.30	1.34	1.38
65 and older	0.20	0.22	0.24	0.24	0.24	0.25	0.26
TOTAL	3.42	3.49	3.52	3.54	3.57	3.59	3.60

Source: Indiana Business Research Center (2024).[22]

ACTIONS FOR PROSPERITY BY 2040

Accelerate digitization of small- to mid-sized manufacturers (SMEs)

Historically, physical equipment and machines make up the foundation of manufacturing. However, in today's context, technology adoption has become synonymous with digitization and the integration of digital tools alongside these physical assets. Indiana's manufacturing sector, with approximately 90 percent of its 9,400 firms being small to mid-sized, faces a pivotal crossroads in its adoption of digital technologies. Despite the clear links between technology adoption, productivity growth and economic prosperity, Indiana continues to lag the national average and its competition states.[23,24] It is therefore essential for Indiana's SMEs to rapidly increase digital adoption in the next two decades.

While the perceived value of digital transformation among SME business leaders is typically high, workforce readiness among frontline workers continues to be seen as a barrier by firm leadership.[25] Many frontline workers within the manufacturing sector demonstrate adaptable, transferable skills and trades for digital adoption, and Indiana's manufacturing workforce specifically, shows tremendous promise.

One example is the Elkhart/Goshen area, which was recently cited as a top 10 metro statistical area (MSAs) for semiconductor labor force readiness based on several factors, according to a recent research report by Lightcast.[26] For 2040 prosperity, business leaders must not only prioritize technology investments but also step-up investment in workforce development and training programs. Both investments must occur in tandem. Key recommendations include:

- **Transform Indiana's existing workforce** through development of specialized Smart Manufacturing talent to drive digital adoption and technological change within firms. This will be achieved through the creation of widely accessible, high-quality education and training programs focused on reskilling and upskilling the existing workforce. An emphasis should also be placed on digital manufacturing skills as they are the foundation for true transformation within a production environment, and include roles such as automation integrators, controls technicians, engineering technologists, and robot technicians.

- **Attract and retain Indiana's Industry 4.0-enabling workforce through innovative work-based learning partnerships.** A focus must be placed on the occupations that are most aligned with the concepts of Industry 4.0. These are often roles that develop, deploy, and support digitization and automation within manufacturing companies, including engineers and engineering technicians, business analysts, software developers and programmers, network and digital systems administrators, and data scientists.

- **Become a national leader in training the AI workforce for manufacturing and industrial use cases.** The rising tide of AI development and deployment within the industrial economy shows enormous promise. According to a recent report by TEConomy Partners and Conexus Indiana, AI is one of the fastest-growing areas of expertise demanded in national manufacturing job postings.[27] AI-related skills and expertise must become more than just a "consideration" in new training programs. Rather, it must be a fundamental component of workforce development. More and more companies will invest time and resources into AI adoption to enhance efficiency and competitiveness. Without robust AI training programs, it's likely Indiana's manufacturing sector will see a major shortage of skilled AI professionals who specialize in deploying AI solutions in an industrial setting.

Grow the future-focused manufacturing workforce by developing a pipeline of top talent, engaging K-12 and offering new education pathways

Indiana is attracting and growing emerging manufacturing industries at historic levels. In 2023 alone, the Indiana Economic Development Corporation (IEDC) boasted its "seventh consecutive record-breaking year" of investments and business commitments that included nearly $29 billion in investments from 208 companies. Many of these investments involve semiconductors and microelectronics, electric vehicles (EVs) and batteries, clean energy manufacturing, and biomanufacturing. The tidal wave of new jobs, new firms and in-demand skills is already impacting Indiana's manufacturing sector. To meet the needs of emerging industries and to generate new opportunities for Hoosier talent, Indiana must act quickly to provide new education offerings, reskilling and upskilling pathways for the existing workforce as well as talent attraction and retention aimed at turning brain drain into brain gain.

In addition to growing the future-focused workforce for emerging industry sectors, Indiana must upskill its manufacturing workforce with a focus on critical innovation competencies, including product design, manufacturing process engineering and servicing of complex products. While large manufacturers have invested significant resources in training programs for more than a decade, it is now vital to provide new education pathways for technicians, engineers, managers and executives at SMEs to transform all aspects of the supply chain. Indiana's base of SMEs must keep pace with their larger counterparts in the Fourth Industrial Revolution to enhance both supply chain resilience and global competitiveness. Key recommendations follow:

- **Develop bold and powerful education partnerships to retain the "Jobs of Today" and prepare Hoosiers for "Jobs of the Future."** While many resources and programs exist to support manufacturers in digital transformation and workforce development, these activities are often conducted independently across organizations and are not part of a connected, coordinated effort. Through the creation of new partnerships among Indiana's universities, community colleges, nonprofits, the national Manufacturing Extension Partnership (MEP) network, AnalytiXIN, and the national Manufacturing USA institutes, regional efforts must be aligned to accelerate manufacturing and supply chain innovation, particularly by providing a seamless entry point for SMEs. As regional initiatives are aligned, they can be further bolstered by federal strategies to support both the current manufacturing sector and emerging industries' workforce needs, such as semiconductors, EV batteries and biomanufacturing.

- **Create regional Advanced Manufacturing Hubs** that align with new industrial workforce development needs and disperse economic benefits more evenly across states.[28] While Indiana has experienced recent success in securing federal technology hub designations (Tech Hubs), including the Hydrogen Hub (clean energy), the Microelectronics Commons (semiconductors and chips), and Heartland BioWorks (biotechnology), more work must be done to explore partnerships with other states facing similar workforce challenges and opportunities, including Michigan, Ohio, Wisconsin and Illinois. To this end, Indiana must engage new partners – regionally, nationally and globally – and particularly with both universities and the private sector in order to position the state to lead in the future economy.

- **Empower Indiana manufacturers to leverage the latest and most advanced manufacturing technologies.** Nearly all products are designed virtually with computer-aided design (CAD) software and many factories are built leveraging digital twin models before they are launched. However, the onset of advanced analytics, AI and machine learning (ML) can empower manufacturers to become more connected and agile than ever before. With terabytes of data from operations and machines, new tools can be deployed to make companies more efficient and resilient. The integration of data and advanced analytics in company-wide operations will require significant upskilling from shop floor to top floor and from finance to engineering and production. Purdue's Excellence in Manufacturing and Operations (XMO) initiative is one example of an institution fostering a broad network that unites physical, digital and sustainable manufacturing. It is spearheaded by the College of Engineering but leverages a wide network of campus partners, including the Mitchell E. Daniels, Jr. School of Business, Purdue Polytechnic Institute, the College of Agriculture and the College of Science. Another example is through better use of university centers that promote education, research and industry engagement with undergraduate business students who are interested in operations and manufacturing management, such as the Dauch Center for the Management of Manufacturing Enterprises. These centers must be leveraged in tandem with large university research efforts to expand learning experiences through innovative projects with SMEs.

Become a national leader in advanced mobility and supply chain innovation for advanced manufacturing and logistics (AML)

Indiana is already a national leader in the transportation sector and has earned the moniker "Crossroads of America." Because a wide range of global logistics companies already operate a heavy footprint in the state, Indiana is positioned to become a national leader in advanced mobility and "Supply Chains of the Future."

Within the next several decades, disruptive technologies could impact manufacturing supply chains, such as autonomous vehicles (AVs) and mobility, advanced powertrains that use electric or renewable energy, data connectivity and analytics, as well as the push for decarbonization. However, industrial supply chains are complex and interconnected networks that effectively work together only when all the links, from large to small firms, perform at their best.

As products and processes shift with the adoption of new technologies and growth of emerging industries, large and small companies alike must open their doors to supply chain innovation and workforce development initiatives. Large manufacturers will likely identify and deploy new ways to move and track goods, whereas logistics companies will innovate and modernize the network that provides visibility, agility and efficiency to its industrial customers. To be at the forefront of supply chain innovation, Indiana's logistics workforce must be trained or upskilled to leverage new technologies and optimize the way today's supply chains operate. Key recommendations include:

- **Train and upskill Indiana's logistics workforce** with a focus on new skills for Advanced Mobility and Supply Chains of the Future. Indiana's educational institutions must train and attract more students with supply chain innovation and advanced mobility expertise at the technical, undergraduate and graduate levels. This will bridge the supply and demand gap for Supply Chains of the Future, including strategic sourcing, sustainability and decarbonization, technology integration, risk management and resiliency and data analytics. Additionally, with the anticipated increase in onshoring of critical products, U.S. companies will need to rebuild highly specialized skills within the workforce.

- **Create a state-wide consortium for supply chain resiliency.** A consortium of industry, academic and nonprofit organizations should facilitate the industry in collecting, consolidating, and sharing aggregated supply chain data with its members. Companies must be empowered to confidentially share key data without fear of competition. Both large and small companies must benefit from the aggregated supply chain knowledge and could leverage it for joint supplier development programs, training sessions, and R&D and innovation projects.

- **Build a "Digital Manufacturing Commons"** to share data, technologies and digital applications that enable connectivity across global supply chains. While large manufacturers have economies of scale to create positive return-on-investment (ROI) for digital transformation and supply chain innovation, SMEs are often left behind. Indiana must incentivize its large manufacturers and OEMs to support their supply chain partners in digital transformation. This will require the development of easy-to-use, off-the-shelf and inexpensive digital tools facilitated through public-private partnerships.

- **Establish a Center for Manufacturing Innovation.** Key industry support organizations, such as the Central Indiana Corporate Partnership, South Bend-Elkhart Regional Partnership and the IEDC, should enter formal partnerships with Indiana's innovation hubs, startup accelerators, research universities and federal funders to facilitate new engagements between corporations and early-stage companies. To drive supply chain transformation, new partnerships must be created between advanced mobility startups, logistics companies, industrial customers, and engineering and infrastructure firms. A new center must be designed to serve manufacturing and logistics innovators across all of Indiana's advanced industries, including the life sciences, ag-biosciences and microelectronics sectors.

CONCLUSION

These recommendations suggest pathways for bold industry transformation through digitization and digital skills, workforce development and supply chain innovation. Powerful partnerships must be the foundation to collectively strengthen and position our largest sector for success in the wake of technological change and workforce disruptions. Hoosier prosperity depends on our ability to make and deliver the products of today and tomorrow; therefore, it is imperative that Indiana seizes the unique opportunities presented by an era of manufacturing renaissance. ∎

ABOUT CONEXUS INDIANA

For more than a decade, Conexus Indiana, one of the Central Indiana Corporate Partnership's (CICP) branded initiatives, has been positioning the Hoosier State as the best place for advanced manufacturing and logistics industries to innovate, invest, employ and succeed. By collaborating with industry, academic and public sector partners on a shared vision for an innovative, skilled workforce and stronger business climate, Conexus Indiana has helped to create opportunities for advanced manufacturing and logistics companies, prepare Hoosiers to succeed in the state's largest industry sectors and maintain Indiana's competitive advantage. For more information, visit www.conexusindiana.com.

CHAPTER NOTES

[1] Douglas Thomas. Annual Report on the U.S. Manufacturing Economy: 2023. (National Institute of Standards and Technology, Gaithersburg, MD), NIST Advanced Manufacturing Series 600-13. 2023. https://doi.org/10.6028/NIST.AMS.600-13.

[2] Tyler Carr, Eric Chewning, Mike Doheny, Anu Madgavkar, Asutosh Padhi, and Andrew Tingley. "Delivering the US manufacturing renaissance." McKinsey Global Institute. August 29, 2022. https://www.mckinsey.com/capabilities/operations/our-insights/delivering-the-us-manufacturing-renaissance.

[3] James Conca. "America's Aging Infrastructure Gets C-Minus On Its Report Card." *Forbes*. July 31, 2021. https://www.forbes.com/sites/jamesconca/2021/07/31/americas-aging-infrastructure-gets-c-minus-on-its-report-card.

[4] U.S. Bureau of Labor Statistics, Average Price: Electricity per Kilowatt-Hour in U.S. City Average [APU000072610]. Federal Reserve Bank of St. Louis. https://fred.stlouisfed.org/series/APU000072610.

[5] "Indiana's Fuel Mix." Indiana Office of Energy Development. https://www.in.gov/oed/indianas-energy-policy/indianas-fuel-mix.

[6] Leslie Bonilla Muñiz. "Carmel-based transmission operator warns of electric capacity deficit over many states." *Indianapolis Business Journal*. June 25, 2024. https://www.ibj.com/articles/carmel-based-transmission-operator-warns-of-electric-capacity-deficit-over-many-states.

[7] Eric Van Nostrand, Tara Sinclair, and Samarth Gupta. "Unpacking the Boom in U.S. Construction of Manufacturing Facilities." U.S. Department of the Treasury. June 27, 2023.

CHAPTER NOTES (cont.)

https://home.treasury.gov/news/featured-stories/unpacking-the-boom-in-us-construction-of-manufacturing-facilities.

8 Eric Van Nostrand. "U.S. Business Investment in the Post-COVID Expansion." U.S. Department of the Treasury. June 12, 2024. https://home.treasury.gov/news/featured-stories/us-business-investment-in-the-post-covid-expansion.

9 "Investing in America." The White House. Accessed on August 2, 2024. https://www.whitehouse.gov/invest.

10 "SK hynix announces semiconductor advanced packaging investment in Purdue Research Park." Purdue University News. April 3, 2024. https://www.purdue.edu/newsroom/releases/2024/Q2/sk-hynix-announces-semiconductor-advanced-packaging-investment-in-purdue-research-park.html.

11 Binghui Huang. "Eli Lilly invests $9 billion to increase supply of blockbuster drugs Zepbound and Mounjaro." *USA Today*. May 24, 2024. https://www.usatoday.com/story/news/health/2024/05/24/eli-lilly-increases-leap-district-investment-for-weight-loss-drug/73835572007.

12 John Coykendall, Kate Hardin, John Morehouse, Victor Reyes, and Gardner Carrick. "Taking charge: Manufacturers support growth with active workforce strategies." Deloitte Research Center for Energy & Industrials. April 3, 2024. https://www2.deloitte.com/us/en/insights/industry/manufacturing/supporting-us-manufacturing-growth-amid-workforce-challenges.html.

13 John Coykendall, Kate Hardin, John Morehouse, Victor Reyes, and Gardner Carrick. "Taking charge: Manufacturers support growth with active workforce strategies." Deloitte Research Center for Energy & Industrials. April 3, 2024. https://www2.deloitte.com/us/en/insights/industry/manufacturing/supporting-us-manufacturing-growth-amid-workforce-challenges.html.

14 Jacques Bughin, Eric Hazan, Susan Lund, Peter Dahlström, Anna Wiesinger, and Amresh Subramaniam. "Skill shift: Automation and the future of the workforce." McKinsey Global Institute. May 23, 2018. https://www.mckinsey.com/featured-insights/future-of-work/skill-shift-automation-and-the-future-of-the-workforce.

15 Matt Kinghorn. "Indiana labor force projections: Slowdown on the horizon." *INcontext*, vol. 19, no. 5 (Sept-Oct 2018). https://www.incontext.indiana.edu/2018/sept-oct/article1.asp.

16 "2024 National Tech Adoption Benchmarking Report." TEConomy Partners, LLC and Conexus Indiana. https://www.conexusindiana.com/drive-industry-success/research-reports/.

CHAPTER NOTES (cont.)

[17] "2024 National Tech Adoption Benchmarking Report." TEConomy Partners, LLC and Conexus Indiana. https://www.conexusindiana.com/drive-industry-success/research-reports/.

[18] Indiana Business Research Center, Population and Labor Force Projections 2025 to 2060 (2024).

[19] Indiana Business Research Center, Population and Labor Force Projections 2025 to 2060 (2024).

[20] Indiana Business Research Center, Population and Labor Force Projections 2025 to 2060 (2024).

[21] Liz Hilton Segel and Homayoun Hatami. "Mind the Gap: The 'Einstein of management' has advice for Gen Z." McKinsey and Company. 2024. https://www.mckinsey.com/~/media/mckinsey/email/genz/2024/03/2024-03-26d.html.

[22] Indiana Business Research Center, Population and Labor Force Projections 2025 to 2060 (2024).

[23] Mark Muro, Robert Maxim, and Jacob Whiton. "State of renewal: Charting a new course for Indiana's economic growth and inclusion." Metropolitan Policy Program at Brookings. February 2021. https://indianagpsproject.com/wp-content/uploads/2021/02/2021.02.10_BrookingsMetro_Indiana-State-of-renewal-sm.pdf.

[24] Charles Atkins, Olivia White, Asutosh Padhi, Kweilin Ellingrud, Anu Madgavkar, and Michael Neary. "Rekindling US productivity for a new era." McKinsey Global Institute. February 16, 2023. https://www.mckinsey.com/mgi/our-research/rekindling-us-productivity-for-a-new-era.

[25] Andreas Kornmaaler Hansen, Lasse Christiansen, Astrid Heidemann Lassen. "Technology isn't enough for Industry 4.0: on SMEs and hindrances to digital transformation." International Journal of Production Research. January 31, 2024. https://doi.org/10.1080/00207543.2024.2305800.

[26] Tim Hatton, Echo Liu, Bledi Taska, and Rucha Vankudre. "Rebuilding Our Semiconductor Workforce: Making the Most of the CHIPS Act." Lightcast. 2023. https://lightcast.io/resources/research/rebuilding-our-semiconductor-workforce.

[27] "2024 National Tech Adoption Benchmarking Report." TEConomy Partners, LLC and Conexus Indiana. https://www.conexusindiana.com/drive-industry-success/research-reports/.

[28] Recap of key takeaways from the U.S. Center of Advanced Manufacturing's U.S. Industrial Policy Roundtable on May 13th, 2024.

5

The Healthcare Dilemma: Anchor or Innovator?

By Bret Swanson
Entropy Economics

Venture capitalist Marc Andreessen calls it the "chart of the century." Perhaps no single image better describes the U.S. economy than economist Mark J. Perry's depiction of wildly divergent price increases across varied economic sectors. Its clarity and implications are stunning.

What does it show? Over the last 24 years, the prices of technology-based goods like televisions, software, and mobile phone services have *fallen* by between 40 percent and 97 percent. At the same time, many highly regulated and subsidized services showed dramatic price *increases*.

What was the worst inflationary offender? Hospital services, with a stunning price *rise* of 256 percent. Medical care services weren't far behind, at 136 percent.

The enormity of the healthcare market contains multitudes: it is the economy's largest sector and source of jobs. Its doctors, nurses, and technologists produce marvels of healing and life extension. It also is the most voracious consumer of government spending and, by some measures, America's least productive industry. These very inefficiencies, however, point toward massive opportunities: healthcare may be the most exciting target for a techno-entrepreneurial transformation, led by AI, molecular medicine, and a revolution of personalized care and financing to counter today's model of bureaucracy and bloat.

Figure 5-1. Price changes: January 2000 to June 2024 of selected U.S. consumer goods and services, wages

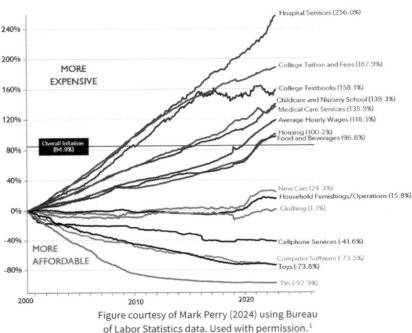

Figure courtesy of Mark Perry (2024) using Bureau of Labor Statistics data. Used with permission.[1]

The question for Indiana is whether it can supply the necessary workforce to meet demographic reality and also transform healthcare delivery and financing in a radically more individualized, entrepreneurial, and cost-efficient manner.

For decades, healthcare has been the fastest growing job sector, a trend that is likely to continue.[2] The Bureau of Labor Statistics projects employment in healthcare, heavily influenced by an aging population, will rise an additional 13 percent from 2021 to 2031.[3] In fact, medical associations urgently warn of shortages of doctors, nurses, and technicians. Indiana must prepare for this surge by training and recruiting large numbers of talented health professionals. The state should also aggressively build upon its already successful biomedical sectors to serve a rapidly expanding global health market (see Chapter 6 for further discussion).

Yet an ever-growing health sector also has a dark side. Healthcare's rapid employment growth is for the rest of the economy a giant burden.

Like all benefits, health insurance is a component of total compensation. In 2023, the average premium for family coverage rose to nearly $24,000, a 46.6 percent increase since 2013.[4] Every dollar businesses spend on inefficient health services is a dollar they cannot spend on paying productive workers and investing in innovation. Governmental budgets are increasingly swamped. The expansion of healthcare thus often comes at the expense of reduced opportunities in the rest of the economy.

Figure 5-2. Average annual and employer premium contributions for family coverage, 2013, 2018 and 2023

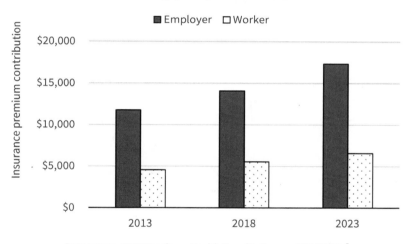

Data source: 2023 Employer Health Benefits Survey, KFF (2023).[5]

Expensive healthcare is a special challenge for entrepreneurs, who operate on the edge and must scrutinize every hiring decision and investment. For workers, meanwhile, employer-based health insurance often ties them to specific jobs, while insurance options for individuals and owners of small businesses are even more cumbersome and costly.

The U.S. dedicates ever more resources to healthcare but often without correspondingly good results. We spend vastly more than other nations – nearly twice as much ($13,000 per capita) as the average developed peer country ($6,600).[6] Yet average American lifespans now trail those same peer nations by a gap of nearly five years.[7]

Yes, behavioral choices and social pathologies skew America's health metrics downward. And for many individuals, American healthcare cannot be topped. Advanced medicine, in the form of cancer cures and miracle surgeries, often delivers outstanding personal results. Richer nations rationally tend to spend more of their economic output on healthcare. However, the U.S. spends far too much on outcomes that are mediocre at best. Why is the U.S. system so much more costly?

On the demand side of the equation, the tax-advantaged treatment of health insurance and the structure and size of Medicare and Medicaid encourages most of our health dollars to be spent through the insurance channel, rather than directly.[8] This "third-party payer" problem boosts prices and ensures overconsumption of many health services, although it probably leads to under-consumption of services not favored by private or government insurers.

The supply side of the equation is similarly distorted by rules and payment methods that discourage innovation. Medicare and Medicaid also mold the structure for most of the provider world because they are such a large part of most providers' businesses. A few large payers – Medicare, Medicaid, and large private insurers – tend to lead to a small number of large providers that can best navigate the payment and regulatory complexity of the administrative apparatus. Unfortunately, the Affordable Care Act (ACA) makes most of these demand and supply side problems worse. The ACA, for example, dramatically accelerated consolidation of hospitals and medical practices into massive health systems.

U.S. healthcare therefore enjoys neither the efficiencies of a truly private market, nor the (often brutal) cost-containment mechanisms of a wholly public system. The result is dramatic over-spending, especially compared to health outcomes.[9]

Many of these effects are especially acute in Indiana. Indiana historically spends a larger portion of its economic output on healthcare than the national average. For example, in 2019 before the pandemic, Indiana spent 18 percent of its output on health versus 16.2 percent for the nation.[10] Several studies confirm Indiana healthcare is expensive, especially compared to its relatively low overall cost of living and compared to its Midwestern neighbors.[11]

If trends hold, Indiana will by the early 2030s spend more than one out of every five dollars – or more than 20 percent of its economic output – on healthcare.

The Centers for Medicare and Medicaid Services (CMS) projects U.S. health spending to rise to 19.7 percent of GDP in 2032 from 17.3 percent in 2022.[12] If trends hold, therefore, Indiana will by the early 2030s spend more than one out of every five dollars – or more than 20 percent of its economic output – on healthcare. Fortunately, a technology boom, which could help transform the healthcare sector from anchor to innovator, is right around the corner.

THE TELEMEDICINE EXAMPLE

This health-tech revolution is coming, but the speed of its diffusion across the healthcare landscape will depend on public policy innovation. Consider the example of telemedicine.[13] For nearly three decades as broadband networks were being rolled out, some had discussed the obvious possibility of conducting more healthcare over the internet. As early as 2015, Dr. Peter Fitzgerald, a cardiologist and engineer at Stanford's Center for Cardiovascular Technology, estimated that one-third of cardiac clinic visits were unnecessary. And yet telemedicine never took off. Providers and insurers couldn't figure out how to bill for non-office services, or to comply with privacy rules, and they assumed they needed special technology instead of using smartphones.

Then the COVID-19 pandemic hit, and everything changed overnight. With hundreds of millions of people locked in their homes, doctor visits finally went virtual. Many patients and doctors found that in many circumstances, virtual visits were a superior solution. Doctor visits are just the tip of the digital health iceberg. In the near future, telehealth might not only save everyone billions of hours of time each year, but also transform health care into an information industry. The chief obstacle to telehealth was our complicated web of health regulations and financing mechanisms, which often disincentivize or even block convenience, efficiency, and innovation. The pandemic finally opened the door to an explosion of innovation. In 2020 alone, telehealth startups raised $10.5 billion in 600 venture capital deals. The question is whether we will allow providers, patients, and payers to adopt the next waves of technology, such as AI, with greater speed and ease, and without top-down control by health systems, insurers, or regulators in the states and Washington, D.C.

FROM ANCHOR TO INNOVATOR

Such rules have blocked innovation and boosted costs for decades. In the 20 years leading up to the COVID pandemic, healthcare productivity growth was nearly stagnant. By contrast, productivity in American physical industries grew nearly three times as fast (though still slowly), and productivity in the digital industries grew nearly *nine times faster* than healthcare.[14] The chart below is the flip side of Mark Perry's "chart of the century."

Figure 5-3. Healthcare productivity's giant challenge and opportunity

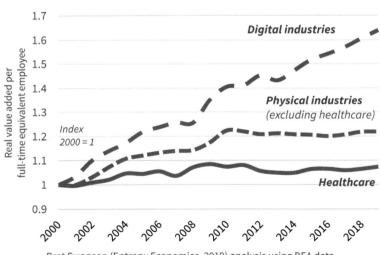

Bret Swanson (Entropy Economics, 2019) analysis using BEA data.

We keep pouring more resources into the system but do not reap more care or better results in aggregate. Under the Affordable Care Act, for example, the U.S. spends $214 billion per year insuring Americans through Medicaid and the exchanges. But as healthcare economist John

Goodman notes, "the number of people without health insurance fell from 15.5 percent of the population in 2010 to 7.9 percent by 2022. Yet...health care utilization across all of society did not increase at all."[15] Goodman concludes with the following quote.

> *"One reason the United States spends more on health care than other countries is that we are obsessive about health insurance instead of health care."* [16]
>
> **– John Goodman**
> President, Goodman Institute

We focus more on financing the existing expensive system rather than promoting an explosion of new, tech-based, low-cost products and services supplied by entrepreneurial enterprises.

Yes, major reforms of insurance are necessary to allow a wider array of individually tailored financial products aligned with consumer choice and frugality. An era of AI dynamism (and potential employment disruption) demands even more options, providing far greater flexibility, portability, and continuity in health insurance.[17] As important, however, we need to accommodate and encourage the onrush of new service providers and technologies that could remake the entire sector. Because of its size, excesses, and slow productivity growth, any acceleration in healthcare's efficiency and pace of innovation could not only deliver better care at lower cost, but also could meaningfully boost the overall economy.

A FOUR-FACETED REVOLUTION

In the past, we have envisioned a four-faceted information revolution in health.[18] It could be a broad transformation of the sprawling industry, consisting of:

1. Smartphones and personal technology

Supercomputers in billions of individuals' pockets (and on their wrists and in their brains and intestines) all connected via broadband networks, will enable cheap, anywhere, all-the-time diagnostic tools and communication and data collection capabilities. Smartphones will be used not only for direct communication with physicians and nurses, substantially reducing office visits. They also will be used as tools to diagnose ear infections, monitor heart rhythms, remind us to take medication, and detect emergent maladies by sensing chemicals in our breath and changes in our retinas. They will connect to a host of sensors and drug dispensers that will meander through our bodies.

2. AI, big data, and social data

With the collection, coordination, sharing, and analysis of unimaginably large troves of specific data about patients, treatments, physicians, environments, and facilities, researchers and patients themselves will dig deeper and make more connections than ever before.

Some of the algorithms at the heart of today's deep learning technologies were developed 30 years ago. But we did not have enough computing power or sufficiently large data sets to make them useful. Now, with millions of times the computing power and data sets trillions of times bigger, that is changing. The accumulation of data and speed of discovery will produce a virtuous circle that will make today look like a dark age of medicine.

One surprising development is that individuals with no medical background are using the internet, which has democratized medical knowledge and expertise, to make significant breakthroughs in their own health and others in their networks.

The Paragon Health Institute has surveyed the numerous ways AI might improve healthcare – from more efficient administration to physician tools to self-diagnostics to deep biological research.[19] Their conclusion is similar to ours: "AI is a multi-dimensional reality already transforming American health care and, thankfully, it has the potential to effect significant medical savings at a time when they are desperately needed."

3. The code of life

The truly radical new understanding of biological information networks, including genomics and proteomics, will yield personalized molecular medicine. Cracking this "code of life" is the most fundamental application of information technology at the heart of the health information revolution – and it is happening. In 2001, the cost to sequence a whole human genome was $100 million. Today, the cost is around $500.[20] "The vital core of medicine," writes Peter Huber in *The Cure in the Code*, "is now on the same plummeting-cost trajectory as chips and software."

Computational bioscience will combine our knowledge of this biocode with exploding empirical data to clear the way for scientists to design new therapies in the cloud. AlphaFold 3 is the latest AI system that can predict how proteins will interact with small molecules and even ions.[21] This could dramatically reduce the cost of pharmaceutical development and greatly expand the number of therapies that can be created and tested by moving medical research away from a hit-and-hope world of trial-and-error guesswork.

Immuno-oncology is just one promising field in which scientists are already designing personalized anti-cancer drugs using knowledge of specific cellular mechanisms and bio-information networks to, in effect, reprogram the body's own defense systems. But it is still early days. Understanding the code of life will also enable us, within the next few years, to begin manufacturing artificial human organs on a large scale.

In addition, 3D bioprinting of human tissue and organs are envisioned for use in clinical trials of new drugs, instead of human trials, which could improve patient safety, reduce costs, and accelerate time to market. Likewise, 3D printing already is improving customization and reducing the time and cost of making artificial limbs.

4. The app-ification of healthcare

For the new health information technologies to truly flourish, the economic model of healthcare must change. Instead of a centralized, opaque, top-down system of big hospitals, big insurance, and big government, we need an entrepreneurial model of numerous firms and technologies (health- care "apps") delivering better care at lower prices to patient-consumers. Healthcare should be more like the smartphone ecosystem – a platform that empowers millions of diverse apps, products, and services created by other people and firms, targeting the needs of individual consumers.

This new model will include Uber-like "doctor on demand" platforms. It will include a multitude of personalized, affordable insurance products. It will promote real and knowable prices. It will encourage far more participation by technologists and entrepreneurs to deliver new therapies and health services to consumers who are far more interested in value. It will mean a far greater focus by healthcare providers on innovation, efficiency, and cost reductions. It will reduce unnecessary tests and office visits. But at the same time, this new model will entail more preemptive diagnostics, preventive care, and health maintenance, rather than post-symptom acute care. For example, some believe that with better early detection tools, we could cure 80 percent of cancers with today's therapies. The potential is enormous, but a successful reorganization of healthcare delivery will be limited mostly by the extent of improvements in tax and regulatory policy.

Such a transformation will require a reorientation of today's workforce. The rise of physician assistants and nurse practitioners over the last two decades portends an even greater expansion and transition from the old model. We will need more diverse specialists as well as health generalists, or coaches, who can help us navigate new technologies and tools in a more personalized manner.

RECOMMENDATIONS

How can Indiana lead the way? Much of health policy is set at the federal level – from Medicare to many private insurance rules to the Food and Drug Administration. But Indiana should engage as many levers as possible to push in the right direction.

- Train and recruit a diverse set of healthcare professionals who can embrace and adapt to a more innovative and efficient health landscape.

- Promote competition, transparency, and the rapid entry of entrepreneurial suppliers of new and more cost-effective medical, financial, and administrative services.[22] Boosting the supply of healthcare – both in the number of providers and their entrepreneurial nature – can through increased competition help reduce Indiana's nationally high hospital fees.

- Aggressively promote flexible, personalized, portable insurance products.[23] For example, allow all citizens to purchase Farm Bureau plans (or other similar "association plans") or plans approved in any other state.

- Promote economic and cultural incentives for personal behaviors known to be the foundation of good health.

- Push federal lawmakers and regulators to ease, waive, or reverse rules – through law or regulation – that promote over-consolidation of large health providers, limit insurance choices for consumers, and limit Indiana's flexibility administering Medicaid.

- Reaffirm the principle of informed consent and once again elevate the sanctity of the individual over the health system. Potent new tools of molecular medicine and AI will present ethical challenges. In recent years, large health systems and bureaucracies mandated indiscriminate, blanket protocols, which often turned out to be wrong, causing widespread health damage. Individual patients and their physicians must be in control.

BETTER HEALTH AT LOWER COST

Multiple advances in personal technology, molecular medicine, and AI should deliver far better health outcomes in coming years. But for these products and services to diffuse quickly through the market and reduce health costs, federal and state governments must better align incentives for patients, providers, and payers. Only then will workers and employers truly harvest the gains of both better health and far lower costs. Lower healthcare costs will not only increase take-home pay for individual workers but also support a more dynamic job market and entrepreneurial ecosystem. ∎

ABOUT ENTROPY ECONOMICS

Bret Swanson is president of Entropy Economics LLC, a technology research firm serving investors and technology companies. He is also a senior fellow at the National Center for Energy Analytics and a visiting fellow at the Krach Institute for Tech Diplomacy at Purdue. From 2009 to 2024, he was a trustee and chairman of the Indiana Public Retirement System (INPRS). Find his Infonomena newsletter and podcast at infonomena.substack.com.

CHAPTER NOTES

¹ Mark Perry. "Chart of the Century: January 2000 to June 2024." July 12, 2024. https://x.com/Mark_J_Perry/status/1811872736064475635.

² Kelly Gooch. Healthcare Job Growth Hits 32-year High. Becker's Hospital Review. https://www.beckershospitalreview.com/workforce/healthcare-job-growth-hits-32-year-high.html.

³ Occupational Outlook Handbook. Bureau of Labor Statistics. https://www.bls.gov/ooh/healthcare/home.htm.

⁴ 2023 Employer Health Benefits Survey. KFF. https://www.kff.org/report-section/ehbs-2023-summary-of-findings/.

⁵ 2023 Employer Health Benefits Survey. KFF.

⁶ Matthew McGough, Aubrey Winger, Shameek Rakshit, and Krutika Amin. How has U.S. spending on healthcare changed over time? KFF. https://www.healthsystemtracker.org/chart-collection/u-s-spending-healthcare-changed-time/.

⁷ Shameek Rakshit, Matthew McGough, and Krutika Amin. How does U.S. life expectancy compare to other countries? KFF. https://www.healthsystemtracker.org/chart-collection/u-s-life-expectancy-compare-countries/.

⁸ See, for example, Theo Merkel and Brian Blase. Follow the Money: How Tax Policy Shapes Health Care. May 2024. https://paragoninstitute.org/private-health/follow-the-money-how-tax-policy-shapes-health-care/.

⁹ Around 48% of U.S. health spending is labeled government – mostly through Medicare and Medicaid. Yet the remaining 52% of health spending is only nominally private. Employer-based and individual health insurance is so heavily regulated, tax-subsidized, third-party dominated, and so intertwined with the byzantine health system that it cannot truly be called private.

CHAPTER NOTES (cont.)

[10] National Health Expenditure Data. Centers for Medicare and Medicaid Services. https://www.cms.gov/data-research/statistics-trends-and-reports/national-health-expenditure-data.

[11] See, for example, this study from RAND. Prices Paid to Hospitals by Private Health Plans. May 13, 2024. https://www.rand.org/pubs/research_reports/RRA1144-2.html; and this summary from Hoosiers for Affordable Health Care. http://www.h4ahc.com/wp-content/uploads/2022/11/Hospital-Pricing-Explained.pdf.

[12] National Health Expenditures Fact Sheet. Centers for Medicare and Medicaid Services. https://www.cms.gov/data-research/statistics-trends-and-reports/national-health-expenditure-data/nhe-fact-sheet.

[13] Bret Swanson. Can Telemedicine Finally Boost Healthcare Productivity? AEIdeas. May 18, 2021. https://www.aei.org/technology-and-innovation/can-telemedicine-finally-boost-health-care-productivity/.

[14] See Bret Swanson. Can Telemedicine Finally Boost Healthcare Productivity? AEIdeas. May 18, 2021. https://www.aei.org/technology-and-innovation/can-telemedicine-finally-boost-health-care-productivity/; and for a more comprehensive treatment of the productivity analysis, Michael Mandel and Bret Swanson. The Coming Productivity Boom. March 2017. http://entropyeconomics.com/wp-content/uploads/2017/03/The-Coming-Productivity-Boom-Transforming-the-Physical-Economy-with-Information-March-2017.pdf.

[15] John C. Goodman. Health Insurance Without Health Care. Forbes. January 18, 2024. https://www.forbes.com/sites/johngoodman/2024/01/18/health-insurance-without-health-care/; also see, Coverage Expansions and Utilization of Physician Care: Evidence From the 2014 Affordable Care Act and 1966 Medicare/Medicaid Expansions. American Journal of Public Health. https://pubmed.ncbi.nlm.nih.gov/31622135/.

[16] John C. Goodman. Health Insurance Without Health Care. Forbes. January 18, 2024. https://www.forbes.com/sites/johngoodman/2024/01/18/health-insurance-without-health-care/; also see, Coverage Expansions and Utilization of Physician Care: Evidence From the 2014 Affordable Care Act and 1966 Medicare/Medicaid Expansions. American Journal of Public Health. https://pubmed.ncbi.nlm.nih.gov/31622135/.

[17] Economist John H. Cochrane has offered several excellent ideas, such as health status insurance, guaranteed renewability, and time-consistent health insurance:

"Options on Health Insurance." August 16, 2018. https://johnhcochrane.blogspot.com/2018/08/options-on-health-insurance.html.

"After the ACA: Freeing the market for health care." June 2014. https://static1.squarespace.com/static/5e6033a4ea02d801f37e15bb/t/5edfd923ac93325534bf13a8/1591728419897/after_aca.pdf.

CHAPTER NOTES (cont.)

"Time-consistent Health Insurance." Journal of Political Economy. June 1995. https://static1.squarespace.com/static/5e6033a4ea02d801f37e15bb/t/5edfd7cfac 93325534becbff/1591728084692/Cochrane+time+consistent+health+insurance+J PE.pdf.

[18] This section is adapted from Bret Swanson. The App-ification of Medicine: A Four-Faceted Revolution in Health. Entropy Economics. September 2015. http://entropyeconomics.com/wp-content/uploads/2016/01/EE-The-App-ification-of-Medicine-2.0-09.15.pdf; and from Michael Mandel and Bret Swanson. The Coming Productivity Boom. March 2017. http://entropyeconomics.com/wp-content/uploads /2017/03/The-Coming-Productivity-Boom-Transforming-the-Physical-Economy-with-Information-March-2017.pdf.

[19] Kev Coleman. Lowering Health Care Costs Through AI: The Possibilities and Barriers. Paragon Health Institute. July 2024. https://paragoninstitute.org/private-health/lowering-health-care-costs-through-ai-the-possibilities-and-barriers/.

[20] The Cost of Sequencing a Human Genome. NIH. https://www.genome.gov/about-genomics/fact-sheets/Sequencing-Human-Genome-cost.

[21] Accurate structure prediction of bimolecular interactions with AlphaFold 3. Nature. May 8, 2024. https://www.nature.com/articles/s41586-024-07487-w.

[22] See, for example, Paragon Institute's research on price transparency. Theo Merkel. Health Care Price Transparency. August 2023. https://paragoninstitute.org/private-health/health-care-price-transparency/.

[23] See, for example, Chapter 9: Health Insurance Regulation, of Michael F. Cannon's book Recovery: A Guide to Reforming U.S. Healthcare. Cato Institute. 2023. https://www.cato.org/sites/cato.org/files/ebookfiles/michael-f-cannon-recovery.pdf.

6

Our Calling: Advanced Innovation for People, Plants, Animals and Our Planet

By Jane Dunigan-Smith, BioCrossroads
and Mitch Frazier, AgriNovus Indiana

Scientific ingenuity, hard work and collaboration comprise the fabric of Indiana's workforce. These foundational characteristics position our state as a leader in human life sciences and agbiosciences. Indiana has unique advantages in these complex spaces: innovative minds and organizations, deep heritages, leading research universities and an ecosystem that embraces problem-solving. This environment has driven a spike in workforce development over the last two decades. And a blueprint that is nearly 150 years old – complemented by bold, visionary leadership today – is foundational to addressing new opportunities head-on. We're at a moment that can save lives and elevate our global position.

But maintaining and expanding our position will require fearless leadership and financial commitments that create world-class training and education – including visionary state-of-the-art facilities. Public and private stakeholders must collectively lead to provide financial commitments, services, and support to attract new and diverse talent to Indiana and retain those who study and train here.

Agriculture and the agbioscience economy make up a signature high-productivity industry in Indiana. Indiana's agbiosciences sector contributes nearly $70 billion in total the state's economy and employs more than 147,000 Hoosiers.[1] This economy extends well beyond farm fields. It includes innovation across sectors of the food industry – from ingredient development to food manufacturing to animal health, from vaccine creation to animal feed optimization. It also includes plant sciences – from seed genetics to solutions that improve sustainability and crop performance. And it includes ag-tech – such as hardware and software to accelerate efficiency and profitability – as well as production agriculture, the cornerstone of the economy, where farmers grow food.

Agbioscience companies are not only delivering life-essential innovations, but also tackling many of the world's toughest challenges. Feeding people, protecting the environment and creating the conditions for a reliable, resilient and secure food system have never been more important.

MEDICAL INNOVATION IS A CORNERSTONE OF INDIANA'S ECONOMY

Medical innovation in Indiana has deep roots, dating to the founding of pharmaceutical giant Eli Lilly and Company in 1876. Over a century ago, Lilly was the first company to mass produce and distribute insulin – an achievement that changed the trajectory of human health.

Today, Indiana leads all states in pharmaceutical exports and is No. 2 in life sciences exports, contributing $95 billion each year to the state's economy. Those numbers are poised to balloon, given the increase in manufacturing investment and the work of researchers across Indiana that is leading to advancements in medications and medical devices that treat diabetes, obesity, Alzheimer's disease, cancer, joint replacement and other conditions.

Indiana's expertise is being noticed. The U.S. Department of Commerce in 2023 named Indianapolis as a Federal Tech Hub for biotechnology – a designation that was punctuated in July 2024 when Heartland BioWorks was 1 of 12 U.S. tech hubs to earn implementation funding from the federal government. The $51 million grant, part of the CHIPS and Science Act, will help Indiana build upon its manufacturing leadership in life sciences and ag-biosciences. Continued funding from key stakeholders – the federal government, private sector and philanthropy – will stand up a research and development ecosystem and help Indiana secure a workforce to meet this important moment.

Heartland BioWorks, a consortium of stakeholders led by the Applied Research Institute and includes BioCrossroads and AgriNovus Indiana, aims to turn central Indiana into a global biotechnology and biomanufacturing leader by increasing the region's capacity to discover and deploy life-saving medicine while advancing innovation that improves the economic and ecologic sustainability of food and agriculture.[2] Further, the tech hub designation can have long-lasting impact, underscoring the state's capabilities and opening the door to new resources that would lead to transformative investments in product innovation, supply chain resilience and job creation.

This raises a critical question: If Indiana is already a leader in life sciences and agbiosciences, why are new initiatives important? As a nation, we face unprecedented challenges. Access to safe and nutritious food, a spike in chronic conditions, and national security concerns with overseas manufacturing risk the health and safety of Americans. Indiana is critical to the nation's food supply and leading life sciences exports. Threats to sustainable production – environmental or malicious – would have serious consequences on our country.

Product development and advanced manufacturing that support human life sciences and agbiosciences offer a big opportunity for Indiana and are critical for our country's health and safety. High-end artificial intelligence and machine learning, gene editing, and digital twins that produce continuous manufacturing must become the norm in Indiana.

Conexus Indiana and Ivy Tech Community College earlier this year announced a new collaboration designed to increase the number of advanced manufacturing firms in Indiana that have integrated digital technologies.[3] The program will include skills training for current and future workers. Indiana also must address industry growth with fewer workers. Strategic and comprehensive workforce training will leverage the opportunity and transform Indiana into a global leader.

The Time for Action is Now

In 2022, one in eight U.S. households (12.8 percent) faced food insecurity, affecting more than 44 million Americans.[4] And the Centers for Disease Control and Prevention indicate roughly 27 percent of U.S. adults had multiple chronic conditions – such as diabetes – in 2018, up from 22 percent less than two decades earlier.[5] The U.S. Census Bureau projects older adults will outnumber children in 2034 for the first time in U.S. history.[6] Despite slowing population growth, the U.S. is expected to expand by 79 million people by 2060, crossing the 400-million threshold in 2058. A U.S. population that is growing and older will require healthy food and medical treatments like never before.

The Risk of Inaction

The U.S. faces a problem that desperately needs solving. High demand, limited supply and manufacturing quality challenges conspired to create a 10-year high in U.S. drug shortages in 2023.[7] Compounding the problem, the heavy reliance on China for critical ingredients in most generic medicines frames the pharmaceutical supply chain as a national security concern.

The COVID-19 pandemic demonstrated the ability of biotechnology to solve global crises. The first FDA-approved treatment for mild-to-moderate COVID-19, bamlanivimab, was distributed by Lilly. Roche Diagnostics was a leader in the development of COVID-19 molecular tests that helped reopen society. And Indiana is the only state to manufacture all three FDA-approved COVID-19 vaccines. But the pandemic also exposed a national security risk: America's reliance on manufacturing bioproducts offshore limits American patients' access to life-saving drugs.

In response to this experience and to prepare for an increasingly threatening geo-political environment, the federal government has set a goal of ensuring bioproducts are both invented and manufactured in the U.S. Given Indiana's advantages that span the bioeconomy, this presents an opportunity for the state to harness the value of its assets, which includes the global headquarters of Lilly (the world's most valuable life sciences company), Corteva (the largest pure-play ag company in the world), and Elanco (the second-largest independent animal health company in the world); the nation's largest medical school and doctoral universities focused on biotechnology and manufacturing innovation (Indiana University and Purdue University); coordinated state, regional, and local prioritization of life sciences to advance economic opportunities; a growing venture ecosystem; and a heritage of logistics excellence, including expertise and the second largest FedEx hub in the world.

The National Security Commission on Emerging Biotechnology in January 2024 communicated the importance of investing in domestic drug manufacturing, proposing the CHIPS and Science Act as a template. The Commission called for government and private investment akin to the $52 billion investment in homegrown semiconductor R&D and manufacturing.[8] That Act's historic investments poise U.S. workers, communities and businesses to win in the 21st century. It strengthens our manufacturing, supply chains and national security, and invests in R&D, science and technology and the workforce of the future. It also will help position the U.S. as a leader in developing industries such as nanotechnology, clean energy, quantum computing and artificial intelligence. A similar approach can be taken for biotechnology products.

Leveraging technology and innovation in development and manufacturing can better position the U.S. to ensure that bioproducts are both invented and manufactured here. The U.S. Food and Drug Administration is seeing a spike in drug applications that use AI or machine learning components.[9] The agency is committed to reinforcing product safety during the R&D and development process while facilitating technology developments. The FDA also underscored the importance of advanced manufacturing in its Framework for Regulatory Advanced Manufacturing Evaluation (FRAME) with four priority areas required to stay competitive: end-to-end continuous manufacturing, distributed manufacturing, distributed manufacturing units at non-traditional host sites and artificial intelligence.[10]

Alan Palkowitz, CEO of the Indiana Biosciences Research Institute, says modern technologies give organizations "the right to operate" and are platforms for discovering life-saving treatments.[11] Precision therapy, for example, targets specific proteins and genes that control how cancer cells grow and spread. And in both research and development and manufacturing, national security is aligned with innovation. "You can play offense or defense or both," says Aaron Schacht, CEO of BiomEdit, an Indiana company that supports innovative solutions to unmet needs in animal health.[12]

Investments that secure a biosciences manufacturing ecosystem are equally important. BioCrossroads, which for more than 20 years has advanced the life sciences in Indiana, estimates that 2,200 to 3,700 manufacturing jobs must be filled annually over the next 10 years to satisfy voids in the sector. Indiana needs on-ramps for early-career hires, support for experienced workers to meet the demands of the ecosystem and investments that fully leverage the state's innovation skills.

ADVANCING TECHNOLOGY: WHERE IT'S HEADED

Technology is critical for human life sciences and agbiosciences. The sector arguably represents the most complex area where we've mastered the least regarding artificial intelligence and technologies that scale up development and manufacturing. Three focus areas – each requiring commitment, investment and workforce development – can optimize ag-biosciences and human life sciences in Indiana:

- AI and Machine Learning, which optimize where and how products are researched and produced.

- Gene Editing for Plants and Human Health. Gene editing can produce increased yields, improve nutritional content, extend shelf lives and offer environmental benefits in the development of plants. Medical researchers can use gene editing to develop highly tailored and targeted treatments for people with unique conditions.

- Automation, including digital twins, allows for continuous manufacturing – producing more products and protecting businesses against natural disasters or attacks.

To fill these voids, Indiana needs greater focus on STEM education to produce skilled scientists who understand advanced analytics and shape our manufacturing ecosystem. Early career awareness through modern youth apprenticeships can lead to well-trained entry-level employees and an ecosystem of lifelong learning. This approach also will hone skills in the incumbent workforce and keep employees educated about technological advances. A more detailed look at Indiana's needs follows.

Artificial Intelligence

The FDA has emphasized the exploration of ways that AI can be used in product manufacturing. A 2023 paper issued by the Center for Drug Evaluation and Research (CDER) cites four areas in which AI may be valuable:

- Process Design and Scale-up: AI models such as machine learning – generated using process development data – could be leveraged to more quickly identify optimal processing parameters or scale-up processes, reducing development time and waste.

- Advanced Process Control (APC): Controls that predict the progression of a process can be achieved by using AI in combination with real-time sensor data. Combining the understanding of underlying chemical, physical and biological transformations with AI in the manufacturing process is expected to see increased adoption.

- Process Monitoring and Fault Detection: AI can monitor equipment and detect deviations from normal performance, reducing process downtime. AI can also monitor product and packaging quality.

- Trend Monitoring: AI can examine consumer complaints and deviation reports containing large volumes of text to identify cluster problems and prioritize areas for improvement for manufacturing-related deviations, thereby supporting comprehensive root cause identification of the problem.[13]

Further, the U.S. Department of Agriculture has set an Agriculture Innovation Agenda (AIA) comprised of four innovation clusters where advances in science are predicted to have a major impact on increasing agricultural productivity and reducing environmental footprint in the future.[14] The AIA describes these clusters in the following way:

- Genome Design: Using genomics and precision breeding to explore, control and improve traits of agriculturally important organisms.

- Prescriptive Intervention: Applying and integrating data sciences, software tools and systems models to enable advanced analytics for managing the food and agricultural system.

- Digital and Automation: Deploying precise, accurate and field-based sensors to collect information in real time to visualize changing conditions and respond automatically with interventions that reduce risk of losses and maximize productivity.

- Systems-Based Farm Management: Leveraging a systems approach to understand the nature of interactions among different elements of the food and agricultural system to increase overall efficiency, resilience, and sustainability of farm enterprises. [15]

Digital Twins

Digital twin is a concept and methodology where physical processes are mirrored in a digital environment by creating a digital replica, or "twin" of a physical system – such as a factory, machine, farm operation or product. Digital twins are developed using advanced technologies such as sensors, Internet of Things, devices, data analytics and simulation software.

Digital twins create the ability to monitor, analyze and optimize aspects of a process in real-time without disrupting physical operations. Capturing and processing data from sensors and other sources allow operators to gain insights into performance, predict maintenance needs, simulate production scenarios, and design and test new products or practices virtually before physical production begins.

Gene Editing

Gene editing is a process used to edit an organism's DNA. It involves making precise changes to the genetic code by adding, removing or altering specific sequences of DNA. This technology has gained significant advancement in recent years due to its potential applications in medicine, agriculture and biotechnology.

Gene editing holds tremendous promise for addressing a range of challenges and opportunities. In agriculture, it can be used to develop crops with enhanced nutritional content, improved resistance to pests and diseases and increased yields.

In medicine, it could revolutionize treatments for genetic diseases by correcting the underlying mutations responsible for the conditions. It could also enable personalized medicine, where treatments can be tailored to an individual's genetic makeup. Similar opportunity exists in animal agriculture, and opportunity abounds in plant science to enable a myriad of improvements from drought tolerance to disease resistance to yield improvement.

FILLING THE VOID WITH CONTINUOUS LEARNING

Advanced manufacturing is relevant only if intellectual property unleashes discoveries, and Indiana has a healthy environment for innovation. The National Institute of Health in 2023 awarded the state $414 million in grants leading to $1.1 billion in economic activity and more than 5,300 jobs.[16] The state is No. 19 globally in biotech patents, and Purdue University is No. 4 among U.S. colleges when it comes to all patents. Indiana University School of Medicine is the largest medical school in the U.S. and ranked 13th among U.S. public universities in NIH funding in 2023. Innovators at large companies and smaller startups alike are discovering and developing advancements for plant and animal health, Alzheimer's disease, diabetes, obesity and cancer.

Reshoring manufacturing and protecting product development will embed security into the business models of these programs. But a commitment to advanced manufacturing requires leadership. One example: The Krach Institute for Tech Diplomacy at Purdue University has launched a new initiative to educate government and business leaders on issues at the intersection of technology, national security and economic prosperity.[17] The Krach Institute aims to educate audiences about key technologies and topics such as hypersonics, cybersecurity, artificial intelligence and quantum computing. The U.S. State Department signed up as the first user. Hoosier innovators also can leverage new opportunities through a $100 million growth fund announced by the state.[18]

But Indiana must sprint to keep up with others around the world. Tens of millions of dollars have been committed to building globally recognized facilities such as the National Institute for Bioprocessing Research & Training (NIBRT) in Ireland and the Biomanufacturing Training and Education Center (BTEC) at North Carolina State. In both cases, biologics derived from living organisms such as proteins, antibodies and nucleic acids – used to treat conditions such as cancer, autoimmune disorders and infectious diseases – are a significant focus and represent a growing portion of drug manufacturing. And regions across the U.S. now are developing innovation districts and training centers to develop talent, attract new investment, and create life sciences and ag-biosciences economies. These collective efforts will foster innovation that will compete with Indiana.

A commitment in Indiana to comprehensive life sciences manufacturing – particularly training and reshoring operations – would elevate companies and sectors, provide new workforce opportunities and address unfilled needs. Lilly has invested a historic $9 billion to construct manufacturing facilities at the LEAP Research and Innovation District in Boone County to support high demand for its products.[19] The broader industry must enhance technology to meet increasing demand while ensuring product safety.

A solution to address industry needs within pharmaceutical manufacturing is already in the works at the William D. and Sherry L. Young Institute for the Advanced Manufacturing of Pharmaceuticals at Purdue University. Purdue proposes a consortium of industry, FDA and academia to focus on sterile injectable drug products, accounting for 80 percent of the FDA's list of essential medicines and nearly half of the new drugs approved by the FDA over the last five years.

The broad goal: create an interactive knowledge base allowing manufacturing challenges to be addressed and new technologies to be collaboratively developed. The expected outcome is a vibrant and sustainable consortium, uniquely equipped to advance pharmaceutical manufacturing and with a record of successful completion of consequential projects.

Many ground-breaking treatments for humans have been developed over the last three decades. But Elizabeth Topp, director at the Young Institute, points out that manufacturing enhancements have not kept pace. Manufacturing medicine, Topp says, is less efficient, more expensive and more time-consuming than it needs to be – driving up costs, contributing to drug shortages and compromising access to life-saving treatments.[20]

Preparing for the next wave of technology is critical for universities, and the industry must ensure that universities understand current and future workforce needs. BioCrossroads is leading work with Ivy Tech, Purdue, Indiana University and employers to understand future talent needs and to develop training programs to address them. One example of this collaboration is Ivy Tech's Biopharma Science and Technology Lab, in partnership with Lilly, that will facilitate hands-on learning for students launching and advancing careers in pharmaceutical manufacturing.

Similar partnerships will be required to address talent needs by ag-biosciences companies as well, and where synergies among human health and plant and animal health exist, they should be leveraged into programs that cut across industries.

Last, an emphasis on cultivating employment-ready students upon high school graduation will be critical to creating a pipeline of talent for companies across human health and ag-biosciences. To this end, the Richard M. Fairbanks Foundation has launched CEMETS iLab, a coalition of more than 100 Indiana leaders working to develop a statewide modern youth apprenticeship system as a solution to the state's overall workforce crisis.[21] The foundation describes the initiative this way:

> *The 10-month Implementation Lab – referred to as an iLab – is an intensive collaborative that will result in a statewide plan to increase modern youth apprenticeships across key sectors. The goal is to ensure that by 2030, every student and adult learner in Indiana has access to high-quality education and training options...Indiana's youth apprenticeship model allows students to participate in a three-year, paid work-and-learn program to prepare them for in-demand careers. It culminates in a high school diploma and an industry credential...The model is based on Switzerland's system, which is the "gold standard" for educating young people and meeting labor market demand.[22]*

CONCLUSION

Indiana stands at a pivotal moment. Public and private stakeholders must collectively work together to provide financial commitments, services, and support to attract new and diverse talent to Indiana and retain those who study and train here. Fearless leadership and dedicated financial commitment will allow Indiana to maintain and expand its leadership position across both human life sciences and agbiosciences.

Now is the time to take action and cultivate a sustainable workforce for Hoosier companies focused on delivering the innovations that heal and feed the world. With a rich legacy of not only innovating but also transforming ideas into tangible products that improve lives, Indiana is well positioned to continue its leadership in transforming global health, food systems and the planet. ■

ABOUT BIOCROSSROADS

Established as a catalyst to advance, grow, and invest in Indiana's life sciences sector, BioCrossroads is an initiative of the Central Indiana Corporate Partnership (CICP). It supports the region's existing enterprises and encourages new business development. The initiative fosters public-private collaboration by uniting a diverse range of academic, industry, and philanthropic stakeholders, all collectively focused on advancing Indiana's life sciences sector. Committed to supporting the growth of capital investments and talent development, BioCrossroads provides support to both existing and new life sciences enterprises, including the Indiana Health Information Exchange, OrthoWorx, and the Indiana Biosciences Research Institute. BioCrossroads champions the advancement of cutting-edge research and development, plays a crucial role in building and nurturing a robust talent pipeline, and is dedicated to establishing Indiana as a thriving hub for life sciences manufacturing. To learn more about BioCrossroads, visit www.biocrossroads.com.

ABOUT AGRINOVUS INDIANA

AgriNovus Indiana, a branded initiative of the Central Indiana Corporate Partnership (CICP), is a non-profit coalition of leaders across industry, academia and government focused on growing Indiana's agbioscience economy across food, animal health, plant science and agtech. AgriNovus Indiana is an effort dedicated to the region's continued prosperity and growth. Learn more by visiting www.AgriNovusIndiana.com.

CHAPTER NOTES

[1] A. Rydeen et al. "Accelerate 2050: A Vision for Indiana Agbioscience." AgriNovus Indiana and RTI International. July 2024. https://agrinovusindiana.com/wp-content/uploads/2024/07/Accelerate-2050_A-Vision-for-Indiana-Agbioscience_FINAL.pdf.

CHAPTER NOTES (cont.)

2 "Heartland BioWorks." U.S. Economic Development Administration. https://www.eda.gov/funding/programs/regional-technology-and-innovation-hubs/2023/Heartland-BioWorks.

3 "Ivy Tech Community College and Conexus Indiana to develop skills training to accelerate smart manufacturing technology adoption statewide." Conexus Indiana. May 1, 2024. https://www.conexusindiana.com/2024/05/ivy-tech-community-college-and-conexus-indiana-to-develop-skills-training-to-accelerate-smart-manufacturing-technology-adoption-statewide.

4 "Hunger & Poverty in America." Food Research and Action Center. https://frac.org/hunger-poverty-america.

5 Peter Boersma, MPH1; Lindsey I. Black, MPH1; Brian W. Ward, PhD. "Prevalence of Multiple Chronic Conditions Among US Adults, 2018." *Preventing Chronic Disease,* Volume 17 (2020). http://dx.doi.org/10.5888/pcd17.200130.

6 Jonathan Vespa, Lauren Medina, and David M. Armstrong. "Demographic Turning Points for the United States: Population Projections for 2020 to 2060." Current Population Reports, P25-1144, U.S. Census Bureau, Washington, DC. 2020. https://www.census.gov/content/dam/Census/library/publications/2020/demo/p25-1144.pdf.

7 Erin Fox and Michael Ganio. "Drug Shortages Statistics." American Society of Health-System Pharmacists (ASHP). June 2024. https://www.ashp.org/drug-shortages/shortage-resources/drug-shortages-statistics.

8 "Interim Report." National Security Commission on Emerging Biotechnology. January 10, 2024. https://www.biotech.senate.gov/press-releases/interim-report.

9 "Artificial Intelligence and Machine Learning (AI/ML) for Drug Development." U.S. Food and Drug Administration. March 18, 2024. https://www.fda.gov/science-research/science-and-research-special-topics/artificial-intelligence-and-machine-learning-aiml-drug-development.

10 "CDER's Framework for Regulatory Advanced Manufacturing Evaluation (FRAME) Initiative." U.S. Food and Drug Administration. November 1, 2023. https://www.fda.gov/about-fda/center-drug-evaluation-and-research-cder/cders-framework-regulatory-advanced-manufacturing-evaluation-frame-initiative.

11 Alan Palkowitz, PhD, in discussion with authors, 2024.

12 Aaron Schacht, in discussion with authors, 2024.

13 "Artificial Intelligence in Drug Manufacturing." Center for Drug Evaluation and Research, U.S. Food and Drug Administration Office of Pharmaceutical Quality. 2023. https://www.fda.gov/media/165743/download.

CHAPTER NOTES (cont.)

[14] Scott Hutchins and John Dyer. "U.S. Agriculture Innovation Strategy: A Directional Vision for Research." U.S. Department of Agriculture. January 2021. https://www.usda.gov/sites/default/files/documents/AIS.508-01.06.2021.pdf.

[15] Scott Hutchins and John Dyer. "U.S. Agriculture Innovation Strategy: A Directional Vision for Research." U.S. Department of Agriculture. January 2021. https://www.usda.gov/sites/default/files/documents/AIS.508-01.06.2021.pdf.

[16] "NIH In Your State: Indiana." United for Medical Research. https://www.unitedformedicalresearch.org/nih-in-your-state/indiana.

[17] Susan Orr. "Purdue institute launches online academy for studying intersection of tech, national security." *Indianapolis Business Journal*. May 24, 2024. https://www.ibj.com /articles/purdue-institute-launches-new-online-academy.

[18] "Indiana Partners with Elevate Ventures to Launch First $100M Growth Stage Fund." Indiana Economic Development Corporation. May 23, 2024. https://www.iedc.in.gov/events/news/details/2024/05/23/indiana-partners-with-elevate-ventures-to-launch-first-100m-growth-stage-fund.

[19] "Lilly Increases Manufacturing Investment to $9 Billion at Newest Indiana Site to Boost API Production for Tirzepatide and Pipeline Medicines." Eli Lilly and Company. May 24, 2024. https://investor.lilly.com/news-releases/news-release-details/lilly-increases-manufacturing-investment-9-billion-newest.

[20] Elizabeth Topp, PhD, in discussion with authors, 2024.

[21] "Scaling Modern Youth Apprenticeship In Indiana." CEMETS iLab Indiana. Richard M. Fairbanks Foundation. https://www.rmff.org/our-work/ilabindiana.

[22] "Scaling Modern Youth Apprenticeship In Indiana." CEMETS iLab Indiana. Richard M. Fairbanks Foundation. https://www.rmff.org/our-work/ilabindiana.

7

Entrepreneurship and Capital Formation

By Christopher Day and Matt Tyner
Elevate Ventures

INTRODUCTION

In 2023, Elevate Ventures kicked off the Rally cross-sector innovation conference by challenging attendees to not idly spectate the future, but become active architects shaping it. In today's dynamic economy, innovation plays a vital role in driving entrepreneurship, creating jobs, and fostering economic growth. We must have dynamic collaborations between business, government, academia and philanthropy for sustained economic and societal growth. Startups are the lifeblood of innovation ecosystems, serving as engines of creativity and disruption.

However, for these ventures to thrive, they require access to resources, funding, regulatory frameworks, and mentorship programs that can support their growth and sustainability. In Indiana, there is a tremendous opportunity to build on the innovation ecosystem, through greater intentional statewide connectivity, providing deeper support to entrepreneurs and a culture that embraces calculated risk. As connections and alignment increase among statewide business leaders, policymakers, academics, philanthropies and economic development organizations, we can realize the full potential of Indiana's entrepreneurial talent and drive economic prosperity for our citizens.

INDIANA'S INNOVATION ECOSYSTEM
TRANSFORMATION OPPORTUNITY

Indiana has momentum in building its innovative entrepreneurial ecosystem; however, it also has significant opportunity for improvement. A few telling data points illustrate the reality that Indiana's innovation ecosystem will demand much greater attention and investment from leaders in every part and sector of the state, if we want to realize our full potential.

- The median annual wage in Indiana is $45,470. The national median, by comparison, is $65,470.[1]

- Indiana's per capita rate of new company formation ranks around 44th in the nation.[2]

- In its success at attracting venture capital, the primary form of financing for early-stage companies, Indiana ranks 40th compared to other states. [3]

The following figures further illustrate Indiana's opportunities to strengthen its competitiveness.

Figure 7-1. Indiana's median annual wage lags the nation.

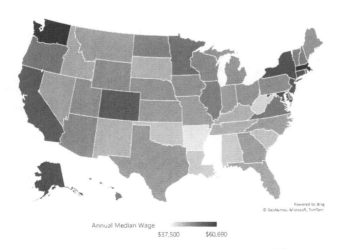

Annual Median Wage
$37,500 $60,690

Data source: Bureau of Labor Statistics (May 2023).[4]

Figure 7-2. Indiana also trails the U.S. new entrepreneur rate

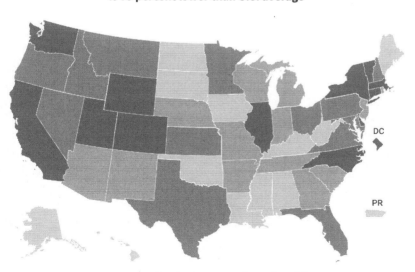

Data source: Kaufmann Indicators of Entrepreneurship (2021).[5]
Note: Indicator captures all new business owners, including those who own incorporated or unincorporated businesses, and those who are employers or non-employers.

**Figure 7-3. Indiana venture capital attraction rate
is 79 percent lower than U.S. average**

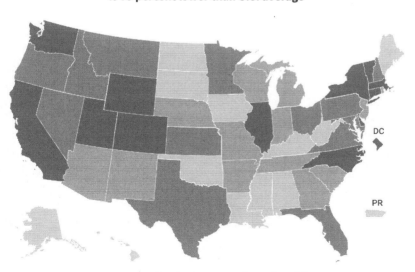

Source: National Science Foundation (2022).[6]
Note: figure shows venture capital attracted per $1 million of state GDP, shaded by quartile.

These relatively low levels of wages, new company formation and investment attraction are significant because the majority of Indiana's new jobs are created by companies less than 5 years old.[7] Why is company formation and venture investment in Indiana low?

First, let's recognize Indiana has many of the core ingredients needed to power a robust innovation ecosystem – nationally and globally competitive in rankings of infrastructure, talent, nationally strategic industries, technology, lifestyle, cost of living, and regulatory environment.

Indiana also has multiple initiatives especially for early-stage entrepreneurs that help drive innovation including Elevate Ventures, economic development "EDGE" tax credits, venture capital investment (VCI) tax credits, innovation vouchers and more. Alongside these funding sources, Indiana has developed its early entrepreneur support ecosystem through intermediaries that improve connectivity and build in-state networks and training programs for entrepreneurs.

These assets have enabled the successes Indiana has achieved to date in our entrepreneurial ecosystem development. So, what are we missing? The next great challenge for entrepreneurship and innovation in Indiana is expanding our existing investment ecosystem to serve companies that reach the growth-stage of their business' lifecycle.

Figure 7-4 focuses on one dimension of our ecosystem – Indiana capital providers – and highlights the void of in-state funding opportunities for companies that have survived the arduous startup and early stages of entrepreneurship and innovation. Indiana has funds that provide capital in the pre-seed stage, seed stage and even some that capitalize early-stage companies. However, we need to do much more to provide growth-stage investment.

By not participating in this stage of the investing continuum, 100 percent of the risk-adjusted returns and the associated wealth creation gets exported out of the state and Indiana misses out on the recycling of those returns.

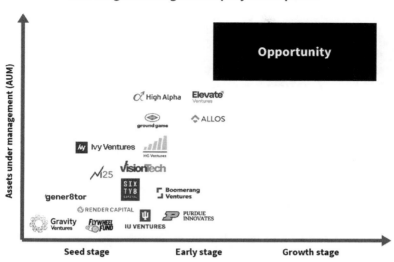

Figure 7-4. Indiana's investment funds do not extend into the growth stage of company development

Indiana's gaps in the growth stage of the funding continuum are not only limited to funding sources and capital density. Elevate Ventures has observed instances where uninformed investors in Indiana have inadvertently handicapped the growth of the companies they invest in by offering investment terms or structures that will be unpalatable to future investors. Leaders in Indiana's entrepreneur and innovation ecosystems need to become smarter about the full lifecycle of company growth and select appropriate capital strategies that ensure our startups are well-positioned for successful outcomes.

Our state ecosystem's shortcoming in the growth stage for scale-up and medium-sized innovation businesses comes with tremendous costs. Fewer companies scale past early stages here because our ecosystem is not built to support them. Fewer talented entrepreneurs come here because they know the state's ecosystem will struggle to support the later stages of their company's growth. Many Indiana entrepreneurs sell their business prematurely due to the difficulty of scaling a company in our region, often referred to as "early exit syndrome." When some Indiana entrepreneurs accomplish the incredible feat of making it to the growth stage, coastal funds are often their only option for capital.

Indiana is currently a leader in nurturing and shouldering the risk of new startups. However, we give scaling companies away to coastal funds, the primary providers of growth-stage company financing. When companies exit for $50M, $100M, $1B, or $2B+, over 90 percent of the returns created are exported to the states with growth capital providers and then those returns recycle into their innovation ecosystems. This does not suggest that we should aim to displace coastal investors. It means that we must participate with them.

The impact of expanding beyond early-stage investing can be seen below. In just one example, using Elevate Ventures investment data since inception, over $175M has been invested over the last thirteen years, and those investments have attracted over $2.2B in additional investments – a 13:1 leverage ratio. Imagine the impact in the next thirteen years if we focus on expanding our investments into our companies' growth stages. Indiana companies could ultimately become the acquirers instead of the acquirees.

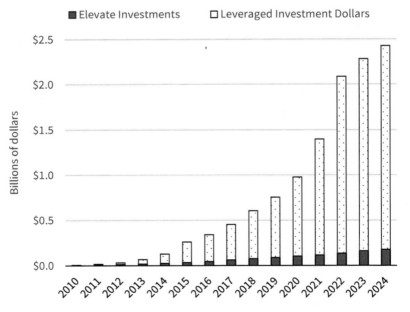

Figure 7-5. Elevate Ventures' investments and leveraged investment dollars, 2010-2024

Source: Elevate Ventures (March 2024).

But today, we miss out on the risk adjusted opportunity to keep investing in our growth-stage companies and the numerous benefits of having more growth-stage companies located here.

This must change.

In this chapter, we advocate for a set of policies, initiatives, and moonshot ideas which can offer Indiana a chance to build unprecedented dynamism and prosperity through the expansion of our entrepreneurship and innovation ecosystem into the growth-stage of companies, alongside other recommendations.

DEVELOPING INDIANA'S ENTREPRENEURSHIP AND INNOVATION ECOSYSTEM

We must think strategically about the opportunity before us. Innovation requires more than just entrepreneurs and investors to make it happen. It requires a complex ecosystem of disparate stakeholders that all have a hand in our future.

In the section that follows, we will provide a high-level summary of key players, describe the imperative to focus on intentional connectivity, identify foundational company building principles, and emphasize the variety of different sectors and areas of expertise that all contribute to our innovation ecosystem. When all stakeholders realize they are vital contributors to our collective ability to innovate, Indiana will undoubtedly build unstoppable momentum.

Figure 7-6 illustrates the key parts of this ecosystem of actors and institutions that surround and enable entrepreneurship and innovation in Indiana. It is a helpful visualization to keep in mind. Consider the assets we already have in Indiana, where we can improve, and the gaps we need to fill. A wide array of actors, contexts and resources contribute to and enable entrepreneurship.

Figure 7-6. Entrepreneurship happens in thriving innovation ecosystems, not in a vacuum

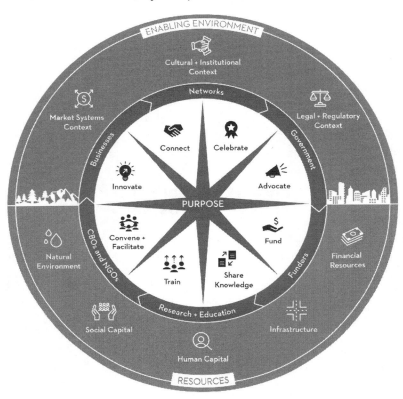

Elizabeth Hoffecker (2019).[8]
Figure courtesy of MIT D-Lab. Used with permission.

CONTINUE AND EXPAND COMPREHENSIVE, FULL-LIFECYCLE SUPPORT FOR INDIANA ENTREPRENEURS

Entrepreneurs come in various forms, each with their unique characteristics, challenges, and interactions within the broader innovation ecosystem, whether they are traditional enterprises or innovation-driven enterprises. All entrepreneurs have common struggles across various types of businesses, including access to funding, market competition, regulatory hurdles, talent acquisition and retention, and adaptation to market changes. These entrepreneurs also have many different types of intersecting interactions within the innovation ecosystem, including talent acquisition, networking, collaboration, access to resources, policy advocacy, and knowledge sharing.

Provide access to funding and financial resources

Access to capital is essential for the success of startups and small businesses. Therefore, we must increase access to funding through a variety of channels. This includes expanding support and collaboration through existing successful public-private partnerships. Three examples that are critical to supporting the statewide ecosystem include Elevate Ventures (both the 21st Century Fund and State Small Business Credit Initiative or "SSBCI"), Next Level Fund, and the Legend Fund Loan Investment Program. Over the last two years, Elevate Ventures has been modernized to enable the management of multiple funds without having to recreate the unnecessary overhead expenses that come with multiple small funds. Examples of this include the recently announced first growth stage fund in Indiana and next up sector-specific funds including agbioscience, life science, sportstech and more. By leveraging capital density and enabling fund management efficiencies, the $225M in assets under management today can grow to $1B in ten years. We have now arrived at the moment where the private sector can be engaged to participate in Indiana's coming productivity boom.

Another untapped opportunity in Indiana is working with our world-class foundations to pool capital with our existing capital to increase evergreen investments. Historically, foundations provide funding in the form of grants. Modern foundation strategies now include leveraging a small portion, 3 percent to 5 percent, of annual giving into evergreen investment mechanisms that can continuously recycle monies in perpetuity that carry out the mission of the foundation. Efficient platforms such as Elevate Ventures can be leveraged for these strategies.

There are also grant-making entities such as the Applied Research Institute (ARI) that award innovation vouchers, Small Business Innovation Research (SBIR) and Small Business Technology Transfer (STTR) Phase I grants, and other similar opportunities. These types of grants assist the earliest-stage entrepreneurs by helping to nurture and prepare them for their first rounds of investment.

Collaborate with regional hubs and centers of excellence that accelerate entrepreneur development

Leverage existing funding mechanisms such as Elevate Ventures. To nurture the growth of startups, establish startup incubators and accelerators in key cities across Indiana in collaboration with the local market, universities and corporations that leverage our areas of core expertise, including healthcare, medtech, hardtech, ag biosciences, foodtech, animal health, artificial intelligence, and more. These centers of excellence have already started to emerge, and others noted here are well down the path in geographic areas around the state, including South Bend, Elkhart, Hammond, Warsaw, Fort Wayne, Muncie, West Lafayette, Terre Haute, Columbus, Vincennes, Bloomington, Evansville, and New Albany.

Northwest Indiana, and Southern Indiana, for example, are well positioned to attract companies and talent from other states with less desirable economic and innovation infrastructure. Lean into the massive wins in the form of three federal tech hub designations in microelectronics, hydrogen energy, and biotechnology. These hubs provide a massive opportunity to catalyze innovative companies that will call Indiana home. With centralized capital, we can be efficiently ready to fund the best ideas that emerge from these initiatives.

Furthermore, we must intentionally connect capital providers with local economic development organizations. This type of collaboration creates efficiencies in Indiana's regional hubs and centers of excellence. These incubators provide entrepreneurs with access to shared office space, mentorship programs, commercialization and networking opportunities. Accelerators offer intensive, time-bound programs designed to help startups rapidly scale their ideas and businesses through mentorship, access to capital, and connections to universities, potential customers, and partners. By creating a supportive ecosystem for startups, Indiana can attract and retain entrepreneurial talent and catalyze innovation across diverse industries.

These initiatives not only drive direct, high-paying jobs but also create an ecosystem of indirect jobs, including service providers, teachers, and more. Below is an illustration of cumulative direct job creation and its impact on indirect jobs. Based on Elevate Ventures data, these entrepreneurship-driven jobs are one of the most cost-efficient economic development drivers in the country. The direct jobs created cost $6,149, with an average wage of $97,000, and the indirect jobs cost $892 to create.

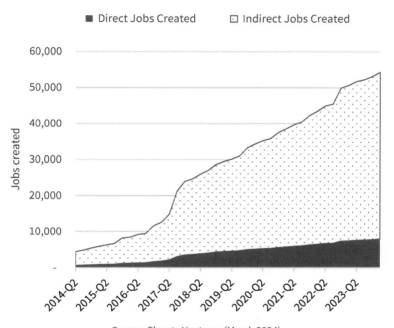

Figure 7-7. Elevate Ventures direct and indirect job creation by quarter, Q2-2014 to Q1-2024

Source: Elevate Ventures (March 2024).

By not fully engaging unique regional domain expertise from our world-class research universities, corporate partners, and existing capital providers in different areas of Indiana, we are leaving a significant entrepreneur acceleration and economic development opportunity on the table.

Inclusively offer entrepreneurs training and development opportunities

Some entrepreneurs believe they can use their strengths alone to transform their ideas into successful outcomes. Entrepreneurship education is essential for equipping aspiring entrepreneurs with the knowledge, skills, and mindset needed to succeed in the startup ecosystem. Therefore, invest in entrepreneurship venture development, education, and training programs with public-private partnerships, universities, community colleges, and vocational schools across Indiana. These programs will provide aspiring entrepreneurs with practical skills in areas such as business planning, marketing, finance, and leadership. Additionally, support initiatives that promote diversity and inclusion in entrepreneurship, ensuring that diverse groups have equal access to resources and opportunities to pursue their entrepreneurial dreams. However, we must remember that innovation does not happen by entrepreneurs and investors alone. It takes a community.

Expand programs that support entrepreneurs directly or mobilize new supporters from the ecosystem

Encouraging rich statewide connectivity through organizations such as the Indiana Technology and Innovation Association and the Indiana Chamber of Commerce to encourage relationship-building with our legislators to share with them the effects of policymaking and how to avoid unintended consequences is vitally important. Open lines of communication between the public and private sectors will enable us to progress decades at a time, mitigate setbacks, and enable productive policymaking.

The relationship between the public and private sector has yielded incredible ecosystem programs, including the venture capital investment tax credit, software-as-a-service sales tax exemption, 21 Fund, Next Level Fund, tax credit transferability, training grants, Small Business Innovation Research (SBIR) and Small Business Technology Transfer (STTR) grants, Indiana vouchers, and many more. Continuing to improve the efficiency of these initiatives will better support our innovation ecosystem's entrepreneurs. All of these directly help innovative companies that create high-paying jobs.

Adopt entrepreneur-friendly policies and streamline regulatory processes

Empowering entrepreneurship and capital formation through a comprehensive policy that fuels the innovation ecosystem throughout Indiana is critical. Policymaking that supports resources, funding density, research, development and mentorship programs helps lay the foundation for a more robust entrepreneurial ecosystem that leads to jobs that pay well above the national average.

Regulatory barriers can impede the growth of startups and small businesses by imposing unnecessary costs and administrative burdens. Therefore, undertake efforts to streamline regulatory processes and reduce red tape for startups. This includes simplifying business registration procedures, licensing requirements, and permitting processes. Additionally, establish a single point of contact or online portal where entrepreneurs can access information, resources, and assistance related to regulatory compliance. By making it easier for startups to navigate the regulatory landscape, Indiana can create a more favorable environment for entrepreneurship and innovation.

Seed entrepreneurship in Indiana's future leaders

Lean into entrepreneurship at every level. Support our entrepreneurs and innovators starting as early as kindergarten. Capital is being deployed today through initiatives such as StartedUP, Rise, Elevate Origins, and others that are creating on-ramps for all students to pursue their ideas. An anecdote from the 20th century illustrates why this is important.

In the 1960s, NASA conducted a creativity test with 1,600 students to find creative geniuses.[9] The results were startling. At age 5, 98 percent of these children demonstrated creative genius. By adulthood, that number decreased to 2 percent. We have creative geniuses in all 92 counties across the state – innovation does not start at a specific age! We can be the disruptive education beacon for not only the country but the world. Valuable initiatives include entrepreneurship programs, school options, teaching techniques that focus on literacy by 3rd grade, STEM education and multi-sector apprenticeship programs in schools for high-demand industries. Our education system must embrace talent of all types no matter what vertical our students may choose and also reinforce that tech companies need not only technical talent but also creative talent too. By equipping Hoosiers with the tools they need to succeed in the modern economy, Indiana can cultivate a pipeline of entrepreneurs and skilled workers ready to tackle the challenges of tomorrow.

BUILD THE RANGE AND CAPACITY OF INVESTORS ALONG THE FUNDING CONTINUUM IN INDIANA

Investors play a crucial role in funding and supporting businesses at various stages of their lifecycle. But all investors are not created equal. They have different areas of expertise and invest at different stages of companies. Examples of different types of investors include angel investors, venture capitalists (VCs), private equity (PE), family offices, and crowdfunders.

As discussed in the introduction, Indiana has a major gap in growth stage capital for scaling ventures. The new Elevate Ventures Growth Fund announced at the Indiana Global Economic Summit is an important first step in addressing this gap, but more work is necessary to offer a complete spectrum of capital and build investor capacity in Indiana.[10]

Offer investor education

Investor education and sophistication is critical. If investors structure deals unconventionally or invest in industries that they do not understand, they can place an entrepreneur receiving capital in a precarious position and threaten the long-term success of the company. For example, an angel investor with experience in real estate who invests in an innovation-driven company and requires the investment to be cashed out with a 2x return in the next round renders that company uninvestable to venture capital funders who are typically needed in the Series Seed and Series A stages of the funding continuum.

Another example is attorneys and investors who proliferate poor legal and financial hygiene by participating in phased funding rounds that are executed through SAFEs. These structures are not founder-friendly as they often lead to more dilution for founders, higher legal expenses for companies to unwind, and companies receiving "silent no's" from investors in their subsequent fundraising efforts without ever understanding why.

Education of seed and early-stage investors to place all parties in a position of maximizing the potential for successful outcomes is important. There are many centers dedicated to entrepreneur training. Indiana's ecosystem needs investor training and education too. Elevate Ventures is collaborating with other angel networks to encourage investor education and hold workshops about best practices for investing in innovation-driven enterprises.

Encourage investor specialization and leverage specialists

As we consider entrepreneur funding sources for intentional statewide and continuum-wide coverage, it is important to consider capital density and domain expertise to maximize results. The deployment of capital is not a zero-sum game. It is important to note that venture capital, venture debt, traditional debt, private equity, wealth management, institutional investment, and other forms of capital management have distinct differences that require varied forms of expertise. Indiana needs excellent investors and capital providers of all types. Public and philanthropic institutions who want to contribute financially to company development in Indiana should leverage the existing investment engines and expertise instead of diluting investable capital into companies by attempting to recreate overhead and expertise with numerous smaller pools of capital.

The infrastructure to deploy cross-sector capital is in place, including our banking institutions and credit unions across that state. There is a significant opportunity to leverage these existing relationships more deeply to maximize the outcomes of deploying, harvesting and reinvesting capital. Public-private partnerships are powerful tools that can organically expand and offer efficiencies back to the public and philanthropic sectors and overall ecosystem. Focusing on the density of these efforts creates capital deployment efficiencies, ecosystem navigation efficiencies for entrepreneurs, and accelerates innovation ecosystem expansion.

INVITE NEW LEADERS INTO THE INNOVATION ECOSYSTEM AND DEEPEN CONNECTIVITY

Promote awareness and buy-in from all ecosystem contributors

In an innovation ecosystem, disparate stakeholders play critical roles in fostering creativity, entrepreneurship, and economic growth. Many of these contributors do not traditionally view themselves as innovators, but they absolutely are. They play a critical role in the evolution of innovation and entrepreneurship. Intentional connectivity throughout a community and a state drives success.

Several examples of critical innovators who interact with entrepreneurs and investors include leaders in education, philanthropy, economic development and policymaking. We need all these stakeholders to start realizing the impact they are having, and could have, on the innovation ecosystem. Several ways they directly contribute include collaboration, partnerships, networking, knowledge sharing, resource mobilization, advocacy, policy design, capacity building, funding and mentorship.

Also, access to world-class universities and research and development is vital to every robust innovation ecosystem. Be intentional about creating innovation ecosystem clusters leveraging the talent that already exists in our research universities and entrepreneurial colleges.

We need to be strategic about leveraging one another's domain expertise, core strategies, and skill sets. We need to think in terms of shared abundance, not silos. By thinking in terms of growth and density, all organizations will win and become stronger. Lean into the organic geographic momentum that already exists.

Cultivate cross-sector relationships and deeper connectivity

Robust entrepreneurial and innovative ecosystems are quite complex. It is a long-term endeavor. Encouraging every stakeholder to act collaboratively leads to thinking in terms of abundance, making educated decisions, being willing to fail, and focusing on their core areas of expertise. Strategic intentional connectivity of organizations leveraging their core strengths whether it be funding density, education, talent, corporate connectivity or economic development is critical to accelerate the expansion of our innovation ecosystem.

Indiana has incredible momentum in developing a robust cross-sector innovation ecosystem and has recently had many large deal announcements. The core of the modern-day economy are the small and mid-sized businesses that create high-paying direct and indirect jobs. The biggest opportunity in front of Indiana to prominently take its place on the global stage is to focus on small and medium-sized businesses that not only drive high-paying jobs but build wealth for our citizens and organically grow into large companies, forming a strong well-rounded ecosystem that supports the best place to live, work and play. If we fail to think, act and execute accordingly we risk continuing to show up in studies and rankings that are not desirable.[11]

Support rural entrepreneurship and small business development

Broadband is an essential component of the infrastructure of the future. Rural communities play a vital role in Indiana's economy, and entrepreneurship can serve as a catalyst for rural revitalization and economic development. Implementing targeted initiatives to support rural entrepreneurship and small business development is a foundational keystone. Invest in infrastructure and broadband connectivity to improve access to markets, resources, and talent in rural areas. By empowering rural entrepreneurs, we can unlock the full potential of our communities and drive economic growth statewide for all. The goal should be that every business and Hoosier has access to broadband. Historically, if you could not move people and goods from one place to another efficiently, then nothing else mattered. Today, that applies to data.

BUILD A STRONGER INNOVATION CULTURE THROUGH MENTORSHIP AND STORYTELLING

Promote and recognize mentorship in every layer of the innovation ecosystem

Mentorship plays a crucial role in the success of an innovation ecosystem by providing guidance, support, and industry expertise to others. Therefore, develop mentorship programs that pair experienced entrepreneurs, investors, and industry professionals with less tenured professionals. These mentors will provide valuable insights, advice, and connections to help them navigate challenges, refine their skillset, and accelerate their growth and leadership. Mentorship programs should be tailored to the specific needs and goals of individuals in Indiana's ecosystem, offering both one-on-one mentoring and group mentoring sessions. Incentivize successful contributors and subject matter experts to give back to the innovation community by volunteering as mentors and sharing their knowledge and experience with the next generation of innovators in Indiana.

Tell our stories

Investing in global-scale marketing to tell our stories both in the state and across the world is critical. People are yearning for great opportunities, and competition for talent is increasing with every day that passes. There are opportunities to make sure our stories reach every community, classroom and individual looking for a better place to live, work, and play. Every year, 80,000 young people converge on our universities. Activating the private sector to work with our universities to publicize the innovation ecosystem that exists all around them in just a 250-mile radius is crucial.

Encourage collaboration across all disparate stakeholders to showcase Indiana on the global stage with events such as Rally, the largest cross-sector innovation conference.[12] These types of events provide global connectivity for our ecosystem and invite others to experience the cross-sector possibilities Indiana offers. Corporations, investors, startups, scaleups, PPP's, universities, schools, foundations, associations and so many others get better global exposure when we all come together to invest and activate our cross-sector networks and ecosystems in one place at one time.

Indiana has the know-how, talent, and institutions to tackle these major initiatives. Visionary leaders can invest in these initiatives that will power high paying jobs and make all of us stronger for generations to come.

THINK BIGGER

At the center of all of these concepts is thinking differently, and bigger – to truly be disruptive in the modern economy. The Productivity Boom is well underway and the core of this phenomenon is disruption of data and technology faster than ever with all sectors. The middle corridor of the United States is well-positioned to be the epicenter, and Indiana is the heart because of the proximity and location of our industries and competitive cost structure. We must embrace major initiatives that will power the future of the world. Here are a few examples we may consider.

Modern Nuclear Power (...and Water Security)

Indiana is well-positioned to pursue fusion nuclear energy and modern fission reactors with its robust R1 institutions including Purdue University, Indiana University and Notre Dame, all of which have strong engineering, physics, mathematics, computer science and informatics programs.[13,14] We also have many more incredible nationally ranked universities throughout the state. The state benefits from a skilled workforce and a thriving manufacturing sector capable of supporting the high-precision engineering required for fusion technology.

Additionally, Indiana's energy sector is active in research and development, with companies and government agencies investing in innovative energy solutions. These resources, combined with strong public-private partnerships, can facilitate the development and implementation of fusion nuclear energy, contributing to a sustainable and technologically advanced energy infrastructure.

Water is also a critical resource that we often take for granted. It has become a source of international conflict. We need to take a proactive approach to ensuring access to our water supply.[15]

Quantum Computing

Other states have already started taking big swings at technology that will proliferate in the future.[16] Indiana possesses significant resources to research advances quantum computing by partnering with our universities which have strong programs in engineering and quantum information science. The state also benefits from tech hubs, providing access to skilled professionals and collaborative opportunities with companies in tech and manufacturing sectors.

A quantum computer in Indiana would revolutionize fields such as pharmaceuticals, enabling rapid drug discovery, enhance cybersecurity by developing unbreakable encryption methods, and optimize logistics and supply chains.[17] Such advances would be transformative for our strong manufacturing and agriculture industries, driving economic growth and technological advancement.

Act Differently

Today's rate of change is the slowest we will ever experience. Words like creative collisions, creative convergence and abundance are not merely catch phrases; they are ways of thinking that unlock massive opportunity. We can no longer think in terms of silos and control. We must think in terms of cross-sector, disparate stakeholders, core skill sets, intentional connectivity and collaboration – all embracing one another.

For example, innovators can no longer build just a healthcare product. Today, a new healthcare product likely involves software, hardtech and healthcare all in one. Companies and individuals alike must intentionally connect and collaborate to bring an idea to life.

We must leverage the national and global leading assets we have that create opportunity across the world. We must intentionally leverage corporations, university research and development, the startup ecosystem, economic development, education, foundations and capital providers to work collaboratively together. We must intentionally extend a hand to create "on ramps for all" in the innovation and entrepreneurial ecosystem.

Natural Amenities Intentional Activation

Indiana boasts diverse natural amenities ideal for enhancing our appeal as a destination to live, work, and play. The Indiana Dunes along Lake Michigan offer beautiful beaches and recreational activities like hiking and swimming. The Ohio River supports boating, fishing, and scenic riverfront communities. Brown County, renowned for its stunning state park, provides extensive trails for hiking and mountain biking, picturesque landscapes, and vibrant fall foliage. The White River flows through downtown Indianapolis.

These attractions, coupled with the state's commitment to making trails accessible to every Hoosier, preserving natural beauty and promoting outdoor activities create a high quality of life. We can attract residents and tourists to enjoy Indiana's natural treasures. Activating these assets with development projects will better showcase them and lead to more people visiting – and staying – in Indiana.

CONCLUSION

Indiana is poised to be a global innovation leader across multiple business sectors by leveraging its strong educational institutions, skilled workforce, robust manufacturing base, policymakers, investors, entrepreneurs, philanthropic leaders, economic development leaders and so many other assets. With a strategic focus on emerging technologies, more intentional statewide connectivity of disparate stakeholders, and activating our natural amenities, we are poised to make this vision a reality. By focusing on core skill sets, fostering public-private partnerships and investing in infrastructure, Indiana can create a dynamic, forward-thinking business environment statewide, and position itself as a hub for innovation and economic growth unparalleled on the global stage.

Empowering entrepreneurship is essential for driving innovation, creating jobs, and fostering economic growth in Indiana. By implementing this framework of recommendations, Indiana can further cultivate a vibrant startup ecosystem that provides entrepreneurs with the resources, funding, and mentorship they need to succeed at all stages of a company's lifecycle. Through strategic investments, regulatory reforms, and collaborative initiatives, Indiana can unlock the full potential of its entrepreneurial talent and build a more prosperous future for all residents. Together, we can create an environment where startups thrive, businesses grow, and innovation flourishes, driving Indiana forward as a leader in the 21st century economy and becoming known as the Innovation Capital of the World.™ ∎

ABOUT ELEVATE VENTURES

Elevate Ventures is on a mission to empower entrepreneurs through investment and collaboration. Elevate is the #1 most active VC in the Great Lakes Region, Top 10 in the United States and Top 20 globally. We invest in high-potential, cross-sector innovative companies with a minimum $500 million total addressable market (TAM) at the pre-seed, seed, and Series A stages. To learn more about Elevate Ventures, visit www.elevateventures.com.

CHAPTER NOTES

[1] Belle Wong, J.D. "Average Salary By State In 2024." *Forbes.* May 1, 2024. https://www.forbes.com/advisor/business/average-salary-by-state.

[2] "Indiana Prosperity 2035: A Vision for Economic Acceleration, Report Card." Indiana Chamber Foundation. December 2023. https://www.indianachamber.com/wp-content/uploads/2023/12/INProsperity2035_ReportCard23.pdf.

[3] "Indiana Prosperity 2035: A Vision for Economic Acceleration, Report Card." Indiana Chamber Foundation. December 2023. https://www.indianachamber.com/wp-content/uploads/2023/12/INProsperity2035_ReportCard23.pdf.

[4] "Occupational Employment and Wage Statistics." Bureau of Labor Statistics. May 2023. https://www.bls.gov/oes/tables.htm.

[5] "Indiana Rate of New Entrepreneurs." Ewing Marion Kauffman Foundation. https://indicators.kauffman.org/state/indiana/rate-of-new-entrepreneurs/2021.

[6] National Science Board. "Venture Capital Disbursed per $1 Million of Gross Domestic Product." Science and Engineering Indicators: State Indicators. December 18, 2023. Alexandria, VA: National Science Foundation. https://ncses.nsf.gov/indicators/states/indicator/venture-capital-per-1-million-state-gdp.

[7] "Indiana Celebrates Small Business Week and the Vital Impact Entrepreneurs Have on Thriving Hoosier Economy." Indiana Economic Development Corporation. April 29, 2024. https://www.iedc.in.gov/events/news/details/2024/04/29/indiana-celebrates-small-business-week-and-the-vital-impact-entrepreneurs-have-on-thriving-hoosier-economy.

[8] Elizabeth Hoffecker. "Understanding Innovation Ecosystems: A Framework for Joint Analysis and Action." 2019. (Cambridge: MIT D-Lab). https://d-lab.mit.edu /sites /default/files/inline-files/Understanding_Innovation_Ecosystems_FINAL_JULY 2019.pdf.

CHAPTER NOTES (cont.)

[9] Rohini Venkatraman. "You're 96 Percent Less Creative Than You Were as a Child. Here's How to Reverse That." *Inc.* January 18, 2018. https://www.inc.com/rohini-venkatraman/4-ways-to-get-back-creativity-you-had-as-a-kid.html.

[10] "Indiana Partners with Elevate Ventures to Launch First $100M Growth Stage Fund." Indiana Economic Development Corporation. May 23, 2024. https://www.iedc.in.gov/events/news/details/2024/05/23/indiana-partners-with-elevate-ventures-to-launch-first-100m-growth-stage-fund.

[11] Deane Biermeier, Samantha Allen. "10 States People Are Fleeing And 10 States People Are Moving To." *Forbes Home.* September 4, 2023. https://www.forbes.com/home-improvement/features/states-move-to-from.

[12] "Rally." https://rallyinnovation.com.

[13] Roberto Bocca and Johnny Wood. "Small reactors could make nuclear energy big again. How do they work, and are they safe?" World Economic Forum. October 6, 2022. https://www.weforum.org/agenda/2022/10/nuclear-power-power-plant-smrs-clean-energy.

[14] Matteo Barbarino. "What is Nuclear Fusion?" International Atomic Energy Association. August 3, 2024. https://www.iaea.org/newscenter/news/what-is-nuclear-fusion.

[15] Elena Bruess. "Great Lakes Water Diversions Could Be More Numerous." *Great Lakes Now.* May 11, 2021. https://www.greatlakesnow.org/2021/05/great-lakes-water-diversions-future-possibilities.

[16] Sarah Mulholland. "Colorado is a regional quantum hub, but what does that mean?" *CPR News.* January 31, 2024. https://www.cpr.org/2024/01/31/colorado-regional-quantum-hub-interview.

[17] Forbes Expert Panel, Forbes Technology Council. "15 Significant Ways Quantum Computing Could Soon Impact Society." *Forbes.* April 18, 2023. https://www.forbes.com/sites/forbestechcouncil/2023/04/18/15-significant-ways-quantum-computing-could-soon-impact-society.

8

Employers as Educators

By Todd Hurst, PhD and Jason Bearce
Indiana Chamber of Commerce

Indiana has made significant strides in the past two decades, growing to become a powerhouse for both economic development and business climate. Long recognized for its prowess in advanced manufacturing, the state also is a national leader in a diverse array of advanced industries, including bio-life sciences, medical device manufacturing, health care, information technology, agriculture, and national security and defense.

As we look to the future, Indiana stands poised to further excel in emerging technologies such as microchip manufacturing, energy development and transmission, and artificial intelligence.

In this dynamic landscape, Indiana's business and policy climate have undergone a rapid evolution. With a laser focus on fostering economic growth and fueling entrepreneurship, the state has become a magnet for innovation and investment. From groundbreaking new projects to thriving industry ecosystems, Indiana is buzzing with energy and opportunity.

However, amid this success, a critical challenge looms large: human capital. Like many states, Indiana grapples with the daunting task of nurturing and fully harnessing its workforce potential. Yes, we have world-class postsecondary education institutions, but we rank 36th in the country in keeping that talent after graduation.[1]

Indiana currently is near full employment with a 3.2 percent unemployment rate, yet employers still feel the pain of not being able to find talent with the right skills to do the job. In conversations with business leaders and economic experts, one question echoes: "What are we doing today to address our talent issues for the future?"

The Indiana Chamber of Commerce has conducted an annual survey of employers across the state for nearly two decades with the intention of better understanding employers' workforce challenges while also identifying potential approaches and strategies to address these needs. This invaluable data allows us to gain deep insights into employer perspectives and priorities, spanning a range of economic environments.

From this survey, a clear and consistent message has been identified: workforce is the most critical issue facing Hoosier employers. While many fantastic and meaningful strategies have been developed, the need is acute and constrains employers' ability to thrive, particularly among small and midsize businesses that comprise the majority.[2]

This reality is reinforced by the U.S. Chamber of Commerce, which has indicated that Indiana has a "severe" workforce shortage. In its report, "Understanding Indiana's Labor Market," the U.S. Chamber states:

> *The State of Indiana has a favorable landscape for businesses and individuals, with a diverse economy, strong labor market recovery, and a robust small business ecosystem. Immigrants contribute meaningfully to the state's workforce and economy, while educational attainment, quality of life, and cost of living factors remain promising... On the downside, Indiana is grappling with a workforce shortage, evident by the fact that there are only 72 available workers for every 100 open job positions in the Hoosier State.[3]*

This talent shortage in Indiana also brings a significant cost to industries across the state. For example, a study conducted by the National Association of Manufacturers (NAM) estimated that the talent shortage could lead to a shortage of 2.1 million jobs in the manufacturing sector alone – a shortage that could have an economic impact in the trillions.[4]

The potential impact of the skills shortage on Indiana's future economic development prospects is of great concern because business expansion, relocation and capital investment decisions increasingly center on the quantity and quality of the working-age talent in each state and community. Talent recruitment has replaced business recruitment as the main concern for economic developers.[5]

However, an emergent reality has begun to be embraced across the state with respect to addressing these challenges. It has become apparent that employers can no longer stand on the sidelines and hope for talent to show up on their doorsteps fully skilled and equipped to meet their specific business needs. Globalization and the rise of artificial intelligence, paired with a new generation of consumers who desire more personal, intuitive brand experiences, are forcing companies to rethink their approach to talent management and acquisition.[6]

Instead, employers are beginning to take a stronger and more proactive role in the talent development ecosystem; whether that is through notifying training partners of their needs or engaging in co-training models. Across the state, employers recognize that in this new economy a critical part of their talent strategy must involve education.

In thinking about the best strategy for addressing this challenge, three pools of potential talent exist:

(1) Proactive pipeline development that begins engaging future talent much earlier, at the K-12 and postsecondary levels.

(2) Upskilling, transitioning and re-engaging the current workforce.

(3) Attracting new talent from outside of Indiana.

In this chapter we will focus primarily on pools one and two; though we must acknowledge pool three is incredibly important and requires significant attention.

This chapter serves to provide strategic vision for why this is an important shift and how it might be a defining solution that sets Indiana apart from every other state. We will begin by addressing what might seem to be a simple question: What do we mean by the term "workforce"?

WHAT IS WORKFORCE?

At the state Chamber of Commerce, we frequently engage in conversations with a broad cross-section of business and community leaders, economic development strategists, policymakers and other key stakeholders. In nearly every discussion across communities and industry sectors, workforce development emerges as a top priority and shared concern. Yet, despite the prominence of this issue, workforce development remains a curiously ill-defined and often misunderstood topic. As noted by Lyn Haralson from the St. Louis Fed:

> *"Workforce development" is an essential component of community economic development in any economic climate... Generally speaking, the term has come to describe a relatively wide range of activities, policies and programs employed by geographies to create, sustain and retain a viable workforce that can support current and future business and industry. Beyond this general understanding, it is difficult to gain a consensus as to the definition of workforce development, perhaps because each user of the term approaches it from a different perspective.[7]*

This ambiguity leads to a fractured system. If one were to scan their local community, they would find their area high school teaching courses aligned to career pathways; higher education institutions preparing future business and community leaders; non-profits supporting individuals looking for re-training and educational support; workforce boards supporting displaced workers and under-credentialed individuals; and local resource hubs providing adult education and English language learner support. All of these efforts are "workforce" programs, though governed and motivated by different purposes. This dynamic exacerbates an often-shared lament in workforce development circles that we are "program rich" but "system poor."

For the purpose of this chapter, we will use the terms workforce and talent interchangeably. We are adopting a universal perspective of workforce that entails a comprehensive approach to development of talent that leads to individuals finding economic prosperity and business having the skilled talent to do their work effectively. This ambiguity of definition does reinforce, however, that there is a pressing need for the state to develop a clear and concise approach to workforce that can serve to govern a complex system, but that topic is beyond the scope of this chapter.

THE ROLE OF AI

Before diving into specific strategies and considerations for the future role of employers, we must recognize that the economy and workforce are in a significant state of flux currently as the world is seeing precipitous technological growth. Artificial intelligence (AI) is poised to reshape Indiana's workforce, with automation and digitalization driving significant changes in job roles and skill requirements.

According to a report by the Brookings Institution, Indiana is among the top 10 states in the U.S. most vulnerable to automation, with approximately 1.08 million jobs (representing 38 percent of the state's workforce) at high risk of displacement due to automation by 2030. Industries such as manufacturing, transportation, and retail trade are expected to be particularly impacted by AI-driven automation, leading to a transformation in the composition of jobs in these sectors.

Concurrently, the demand for AI-related skills is on the rise in Indiana. Data from TechPoint, an Indiana-based initiative focused on tech-enabled industries, indicates that the pace of AI adoption is growing rapidly and has the potential to affect nearly every role. Furthermore, TechPoint's research has found that there is widespread agreement that there is and will be a need for more professional development and training by the current workforce to understand and implement AI effectively, but there is little clarity on where that training exists and what is most valuable at the moment.

The rise of AI demonstrates how technological innovation can transform the way industries function. Some fear that AI will lead to mass layoffs and restructure the way American society functions at its core.[8] Others believe it will increase productivity and growth and lead to more employment opportunities.[9] The truth is likely a combination of both, but effectively navigating this new world requires employers to be much more engaged in the system. This greater engagement includes rethinking the role of industry not only regarding education and training but also how companies interact with the state. Industry must reimagine how to send clear signals to the state about where the labor market and economic opportunities are heading. The strategies for how we might facilitate this restructuring are the subject of our next section.

STRATEGIES

What is needed is a paradigm shift. A shift that moves employers away from being reactive consumers of the state's workforce ecosystem to fully engaged partners, immersed in the state's education-to-workforce ecosystem as collaborative co-developers of Hoosier talent. While complex, the seeds of this change already have begun to take root.

It is worth noting that "employers as educators" is by no means a new or novel concept from a historical perspective. Industries have long been highly engaged in the training of their workforce. Since the late 13th century, industry guilds and apprenticeship programs were a staple of industry practice and served as the primary mechanism for building talent pipelines.

In our modern era, however, especially in America, we have outsourced talent development – expecting the education system to fulfill all of the requirements for employers. This strategy might find success in times of high unemployment and a loose labor market, but in today's landscape it is impractical. As was recently shared in a U.S. Chamber of Commerce meeting, "You don't see employers place a *'raw steel wanted'* sign outside of their businesses when their raw material supply chain breaks down; why do we do that when our talent supply chain does?"

Systemic Change

"Employer-led" and "demand-driven" have become commonplace buzzwords among policymakers and programmatic leaders looking to align education and training offerings with workforce needs. The intent behind adopting employer-driven strategies is laudable and directionally correct. Where many of these ideas fall short, however, is in the deployment of that concept in a structured and sustainable way. In most cases, programs are developed by well-meaning and knowledgeable government servants or non-profit leaders, and employers are occasionally brought in at strategic points to provide feedback or guidance on the work that is being developed. While understandable, that is hardly employer-led or demand-driven.

Such a misaligned system is not created intentionally. It is in many cases the only way to approach workforce problems because of two distinct challenges that confront the system: 1) employers are exceedingly busy and, due to past experience, often reticent to dedicate the time and resources needed to address these complex issues; and 2) there is not a coordinated system or shared approach for engaging employers regularly, consistently or systematically, which creates confusion and frustration as employers are overwhelmed and become frustrated by the sheer volume and variety of requests directed at them. A business leader's main driver is profitability, and every new meeting or time commitment is a calculated investment with the bottom line in mind.

As we look to the future, we must acknowledge that having employers as clear partners in our education and training ecosystem is incredibly important. This is not a revolutionary concept. In the mid-1990s, McTighe and Wiggin's *Understanding by Design* proposed that all curriculum development should incorporate a backward design mentality. They suggested that educators should begin with a goal of what they want students to learn and then structure their content to ensure students reach that goal. This approach can be applied to workforce and talent issues. Planning for a student's pathway should begin with the goal of what is necessary for them to be successful in work and life. Logically, those that hire students and create opportunities – employers – must be engaged in defining that end goal.

To enable such an approach, though, we must change the way that the non-profit sector and government engage. This is not simply a process-oriented change, but a systemic shift in the role of business and employers. It is a model that can be found in the way the Swiss have approached their talent needs.

The Swiss Model

There has been a great deal of attention paid to the Swiss model as they have dramatically shifted their talent development systems over the last 30 years. It is important to note that we cannot expect to recreate this system fully because of systemic, cultural, and economic differences. However, there are structural elements that are valuable models for how we might redesign employer demand signaling to the education system in the coming decade.

The Swiss apprenticeship system is recognized the world over as a model for career alignment and preparation that both meets the needs of the individual and industry. Underlying their programmatic effort, however, is a structural approach to industry engagement unlike anything in America. Swiss business and industry associations play a crucial role in informing skills and curriculum development by providing industry-specific expertise and insights. These associations – representing various sectors such as manufacturing, finance, and technology – serve as authoritative bodies that understand the evolving demands of their respective industries. Through regular communication with members and stakeholders, they gather data on emerging trends, technological advancements, and skill requirements.

The Swiss accomplish this through leveraging their national and regional business associations, so that they work collectively to coordinate activities and goals. Each partner has a clear role and responsibility, and partners work in concert with each other. Using this information, Swiss associations contribute to the design and refinement of educational curricula. They collaborate with educational institutions to ensure that vocational and academic programs incorporate the latest industry standards and practices. By offering input on curriculum development, these associations help bridge the gap between theoretical learning and practical application, ensuring that graduates are equipped with the skills needed to excel in the workforce. The result is a system that is nimble and responsive to industry needs but also flexible enough to allow for the choices and needs of the individual.

The Hoosier Model

As noted before, we cannot simply lift the Swiss employer framework and place it in Indiana. There are cultural and societal differences that do not make the models a one-to-one corollary. We can, however, consider the core elements of this model and create a uniquely Hoosier solution. Creating a system that moves employers away from reactive participation to proactive demand signaling would be an incredibly positive development.

Our vision for the future includes a system in which employers are organized and see value in leveraging their industry association and sector partnerships to take on talent development in a coordinated way. This would enable a more streamlined approach to the state's challenges and would also allow all businesses to have the same access to talent regardless of size or location.

Secondarily, through the above framework, we feel it is critically important that employers become the demand signal to the state in terms of skill and competency identification, credentials of demand, and talent projections. More importantly, the state must have processes in place to meaningfully respond to that demand signal with clear assurances how this feedback will be incorporated and used by state leaders and education and training providers.

Our current system, which is largely reliant on state leaders establishing solutions and seeking feedback from employers, will fundamentally need to shift, and that requires relinquishing power. We are encouraged that the current leaders of the state agencies are philosophically in alignment with this need, but we must codify some of these strategies to ensure the Hoosier Model that we create has staying power regardless of administration.

PROGRAMMATIC CHANGE

While channeling more direct input from employers into the education system is important, it is also important for Indiana's programmatic workforce offerings to adapt as well. For employers to take on a greater role in education, future and current talent must be better engaged with education and training opportunities that result in recognizable skills, credentials, and career advancement opportunities. In this section, we will outline a few ideas that will define a new way of thinking about talent for Hoosier employers of the future.

In 1963, Bill Cook began a small medical device company that would grow to be an industry-leading, global firm based in Bloomington, Indiana. The story of Cook Medical is one of entrepreneurship and innovation that is deeply rooted in community development and human ties. Furthermore, Cook understood from the beginning that employment was more than a simple transactional relationship: it was a core component of the social structure that supported the community.

Today, Cook Medical is led by an equally forward-thinking leader in Pete Yonkman, who has carried this torch further. Like many other companies across the state, Cook recognized their largest impediment to growth was the lack of skilled talent and readily available workforce. Across the region of southwest central Indiana, more than 29,000 adults lacked a high school diploma or equivalency.[10,11] Cook's solution to this challenge was to embrace a role as educator. Not in a traditional sense, but rather Cook recognized and acted on its power and ability to provide individuals with a job, access to educational attainment opportunities, and space to focus on education and succeed.

> *"The best thing you can do for someone is give them an education and a job."* [12]

> **–Bill Cook**
> Founder, Cook Group

What emerged was My Cook Pathway, an effort that recognizes the transformational role that an employer can have when it embraces its role as a pathway for educational attainment. Remarkably, Cook's approach did not require a massive amount of investment or structural changes to the company. In many ways, Cook repackaged offerings available through internal or state programming and paired them with flexible working conditions. The success of the program has been a result of a shift in thinking; company leaders and employees have come to understand the value of education and that Cook is willing to help advance educational attainment.

The story of Cook is unique in that they are passionate champions for their role as educators within the community. At the same time, Cook's increased engagement in education is a rational and practical response to a clear business problem. Talent was a challenge, yet the community has a large pool of untapped talent on the sidelines. Leaders then identified existing programming, both internal and external, that could develop that talent quickly.

Cook's focus is clear: to empower adults without a high school diploma. More than 450,000 Hoosiers, comprising nearly 10 percent of the working-age population, belong to this group. [13] Other chronically underemployed populations can be similarly engaged and equipped as productive participants in Indiana's workforce with the right employer-led support in place, including individuals with disabilities, those involved with the criminal justice system, immigrant populations, and individuals who have a high school diploma but no post-secondary certificate.

One way that we must change as a state is to truly embrace the role of employers as co-creators of talent. That means employers must begin to recognize that regardless of how efficient the education and workforce ecosystem is, there is no scenario in which any employer can expect all candidates to show up "ready to go" on day one with no additional training or support. Furthermore, even if that were a possibility, the rate of technological change and individuals' desire for growth and development would still necessitate employer involvement.

To this end, it is not just a question of how employers are showing up in the talent development system. It is also important to consider how they are developing and supporting programmatic offerings as part of the future system. In this section, we will look at two specific programmatic offerings that are critical to employer engagement in the future.

New Talent Strategies

Not every company has to go as far as Cook in developing a comprehensive talent strategy. However, every company should begin considering how strategic work-based learning approaches might become part of their talent development strategy. Work-based learning serves two critical purposes for the state:

(1) It connects employers to potential sources of talent and enables the development of that talent in a real-world context.

(2) It connects students to career opportunities, reinforces classroom learning through relevant application of essential skills, and increases the probability that students will choose to stay and work in Indiana.

To the first point, we must continue to shift away from considering work-based learning experiences as corporate social responsibility exercises. They must be purposeful activities that align with a strategic approach to building an industry's talent pipeline. This does not mean that every experience needs to have an immediate return on investment; in fact, most will not. These types of experiences require time and effort and often marginally improve productivity in the near-term. But the long-term benefit must be kept front of mind.

We are concerned that policy pressures will force the expansion of these kinds of opportunities before the mindset of employers has shifted. By increasing pressure to funnel more and more students into worked-based learning experiences with the goal of credential completion, we are asking employers to participate in these programs in response to an external need rather than by embracing the talent pipeline potential and signaling their business needs.

The imperative to retain talent in Indiana is also a significant reason for employers to engage in talent co-creation through work-based learning. Indiana does a great job of attracting students into Indiana's higher education institutions, ranking 9th nationally and behind only Ohio in the Midwest.[14] We struggle mightily, however, in keeping that talent in Indiana. Based on data from the *2021 American Community Survey*, Indiana ranks 36th in the nation in terms of net talent retainment of 25- to 35-year-olds with an associate degree or higher when considering birthplace of residency, not migration.[15]

Work-based learning is a strategic approach to reversing this reality. Without meaningful engagement, our Hoosier graduates, both secondary and postsecondary, do not know what type of opportunities exist for them in the state. Even if students do not ultimately work long-term for the specific employer they intern with, they will begin to make connections and see opportunities in Indiana.

This can be even further developed when intermediaries play an active role in ensuring these opportunities increase awareness of other potential avenues for employment. For example, in various parts of the state (e.g., Bloomington, Indianapolis, Fort Wayne, Terre Haute, South Bend) there are efforts to ensure that students participating in work-based learning activities are treated to special events, connect with local leaders, and become aware of the other industries and employers in the region. Unfortunately, these kinds of events are often funded through philanthropic or one-time grant dollars; it is our hope that through the development of more robust industry talent strategies that these kinds of activities will find more stable support.

CONSIDERATIONS TO KEEP IN MIND

We have outlined a vision in which employers embrace their roles as co-developers of talent. This requires purposeful shifts in the structure developed to support and engage employers and for employers to think differently about how they deploy efforts targeted at talent. We acknowledge, however, that these recommendations are made in a world of ideal scenarios. Reality is not so kind. Therefore, in this last section we will consider challenges that must be addressed and potential next steps.

Equal participation for all industry

While Indiana is home to many industry-leading, multinational corporations, the lifeblood of Indiana's economy is small-to-mid size businesses. In fact, 99.4 percent of all businesses in Indiana are considered small.[16] Despite that over 1 million Hoosiers are employed by small businesses, such companies often lack designated staff or resources to focus on talent development as a core component of their work.[17]

It is for these businesses in particular that a focus on industry-representative groups is critical. For a small manufacturing firm, developing an apprenticeship program alone might be infeasible. Engaging as a partner with a larger coalition of manufacturing firms is, however, strategic and achievable. As the state moves forward with this concept of employers as co-creators of talent, it will be essential to ensure that the voice of these small businesses (and geographically dispersed businesses) are included as an equal partner. We must not create a system that serves the needs of only the largest companies.

Additional critical stakeholders to address include businesses engaged in social infrastructure and hospitality industries. Roles in these industries can sometimes be more difficult to plan for given their typically low wages. If we are not strategic, however, in considering how we are incorporating the needs of childcare businesses, restaurants, entertainment venues, and the like into our overall approach of talent development, then we will continue to see consequences for quality of place, which has long-term ramifications for talent attraction and retention.

Sustainable Intermediary Infrastructure

A second consideration that must be addressed to support the employer as educator concept is how the state will develop and sustain the intermediary network across Indiana. The word "intermediary" is a complex term that is often misunderstood and mischaracterized. Across the state there is a complex network of governmental and non-profit entities that help employers navigate the talent development system. These organizations can take the form of workforce development boards, local economic development or chambers of commerce, regional non-profits such as the Northeast Indiana Regional Partnership or Regional Opportunity Initiatives (ROI).

There is an overall lack of coordination among these entities due in part to the different governance processes supporting them. What they all have in common, however, is that they all work closely with industries within their communities and region, and talent is often the primary, if not sole, focus of their work. While well-intentioned and incredibly important contributors to the ecosystem, these types of intermediaries have grown so much in number and sheer volume of activity that their efforts can overwhelm and often confuse employers.

As we look to the future, it will be important for the state to create an approach that formally recognizes these intermediaries and provides support, professional development, and sustainability to their efforts. We believe a statewide entity like the Chamber of Commerce is a key partner in establishing this approach, particularly since the key goal for these entities includes how we engage employers and grow our industry sectors. Using a framework like "Talent Pipeline Management" from the U.S. Chamber of Commerce, we can create an ecosystem of high-functioning intermediaries that streamlines and supports higher engagement from industry.[18]

Recognition of Promising Practices

Our last consideration examines promising practices. As noted earlier in the Cook reference, we know that there are pockets of innovation in talent development across the state that go largely unnoticed. As a state, we do a poor job of identifying those ideas and sharing them more broadly for replication and scaling across the state. If we are going to redefine the way our employers engage and serve as co-creators of talent, we will have to provide examples and models that work for businesses of varying sizes and locations. In an ideal world, when the update to this chapter is being written in 10 years, we would have so many examples of employer innovation that we will not be able to choose a single example.

One concrete strategy for beginning to catalog such employers is to embrace a call-to-action and pledge around the importance of employers' role in education. Kentucky recently launched a program called "Education First Employers."[19] This program is intended to recognize employers who have committed to offering tuition benefits, flexible schedules, competitive wages, etc. The program serves as a tangible signal of a mutually beneficial compact between employers and employees. Indiana should consider something similar but expand it beyond a marketing and communication platform to include incentives and benefits to employers to make this commitment. Through this, we can elevate concrete examples and models of employers walking the talk and give other employers a playbook to emulate.

CONCLUSION

The overarching insight that we should take away from the last three decades of workforce development is that guessing about future talent needs is not a strategy. To create a system that is aligned with real-world needs and is designed to lead to greater economic prosperity for individuals, employers and the state, we need to engage the end-users of that system more effectively: the employers.

Our vision for the future is to create a system that allows for employer signaling to be more strategically integrated and create an environment that encourages and supports a more active role for employers in educating their workforce. Employers are best positioned to motivate and support their employees' pursuit of educational attainment and skill attainment. This is supported by surveys of employees about their greatest influences in pursuing education opportunities: employers' opinions are second only to family and friends.

Embracing a world in which employers play this more proactive role will require a shift from state leaders and non-profit partners, but we believe it will happen with or without their engagement. In the new economy, employers recognize that education and training is no longer purely an employee benefit but rather an operational necessity that is part of a cohesive talent pipeline and employee retention strategy. ∎

ABOUT THE INDIANA CHAMBER OF COMMERCE

The Indiana Chamber works to "cultivate a world-class environment which provides economic opportunity and prosperity for the people of Indiana and their enterprises." We do that by partnering with 25,000 members and investors, on behalf of more than a million Hoosiers. Formed in 1922, the Indiana Chamber is the largest, broad-based business advocacy group in the state, representing businesses of all types and sizes throughout Indiana. Our legislative action team is the voice for pro-jobs, pro-economy public policies at the Statehouse and in Congress. We have full-time legislative experts in the areas of tax and public finance, education and congressional affairs, environment and energy, economic development, small business and technology, plus labor relations, civil justice, and health care and workplace safety.

CHAPTER NOTES

[1] American Community Survey. United States Census Bureau. 2024. https://www.census.gov/programs-surveys/acs.

[2] In the most recent survey, 74% of Indiana business leaders indicated talent is the single largest issue confronting their business.

[3] Stephanie Ferguson, Makinizi Hoover, and Isabella Lucy. "Understanding Indiana's Labor Market." U.S. Chamber of Commerce. 2023. https://www.uschamber.com/workforce/understanding-indiana-labor-market?state=in.

[4] "2.1 Million Manufacturing Jobs Could Go Unfilled by 2030." National Association of Manufacturers (NAM). May 2021. https://nam.org/2-1-million-manufacturing-jobs-could-go-unfilled-by-2030-13743/?stream=workforce.

[5] Phillip Powell and Riley Zipper. "Making the Indianapolis Workforce More Competitive." *Indiana Business Review*. Volume 98, No. 3 (2024). https://www.ibrc.indiana.edu/ibr/2023/special/article2.html.

[6] Margaret Rogers. "A better way to develop talent." *Harvard Business Review*. January 20, 2020. https://hbr.org/2020/01/a-better-way-to-develop-and-retain-top-talent.

[7] Lyn Haralson. "What is Workforce Development?" Federal Reserve Bank of St. Louis. April 1, 2010. https://www.stlouisfed.org/publications/bridges/spring-2010/what-is-workforce-development.

CHAPTER NOTES (cont.)

[8] Faisal Islam. "AI 'Godfather' Says Universal Basic Income will be Needed." *BBC*. May 18, 2024. https://www.bbc.com/news/articles/cnd607ekl99o.

[9] Emil Skandul. "AI Will Radically Reshape Job Market, Global Economy, Employee Productivity." *Business Insider*. August 14, 2023. https://www.businessinsider.com/ai-radically-reshape-job-market-global-economy-employee-labor-innovation-2023-8.

[10] A region that has since come to be referred to as the Indiana Uplands.

[11] Pete Yonkman. "IAACE Presentation." 2018. https://iaace.com/wp-content/uploads/2018/12/a_different_approach_to_adult_education_peteyonkman_cookgroup_4_25_2018_optimized.pdf.

[12] Pete Yonkman. "IAACE Presentation." 2018.

[13] Lightcast, 2024.

[14] "Table 309.10. Residence and migration of all first-time degree/certificate-seeking undergraduates in degree-granting postsecondary institutions, by state or jurisdiction: Fall 2020." National Center for Education Statistics. 2020. https://nces.ed.gov/programs/digest/d21/tables/dt21_309.10.asp?current=yes.

[15] "American Community Survey." United States Census Bureau. 2024. https://www.census.gov/programs-surveys/acs.

[16] "Indiana Small Business Economic Profile." U.S. Small Business Administration, Office of Advocacy. 2022. https://advocacy.sba.gov/wp-content/uploads/2022/08/Small-Business-Economic-Profile-IN.pdf.

[17] "Indiana Small Business Economic Profile." U.S. Small Business Administration, Office of Advocacy. 2022. https://advocacy.sba.gov/wp-content/uploads/2022/08/Small-Business-Economic-Profile-IN.pdf.

[18] "Talent Pipeline Management." U.S. Chamber of Commerce. 2024. https://www.uschamberfoundation.org/solutions/workforce-development-and-training/talent-pipeline-management.

[19] "Education First Employers." Kentucky Community and Technical College System. 2024. https://kctcs.edu/efe/index.aspx.

9

Where, How and Why People Work

By Brad Rhorer and Laura Miller
Ascend Indiana

If the COVID-19 pandemic taught us anything about the future of work it was this: where, how and why people work can change dramatically and with little warning. It also demonstrated that we must be prepared to adjust to outside forces that jeopardize our economy. Whether employees set up offices at home or businesses kept operations rolling with essential workers onsite, Indiana's economy kept moving, and we emerged with new insights that will carry us well into the future.

The 2022 report *Indiana's Evolving Labor Market* issued by Ascend Indiana and EmployIndy showed that highly skilled and educated workers were most in demand.[1] The message was clear that as the labor market continues to change at a rapid pace, it is more important than ever to retain people with relevant knowledge and skills and to recruit more to our state to meet the needs and job opportunities of employers.

The report further noted that "this highlights the increasing importance of long-standing macroeconomic trends related to globalization (and now onshoring), automation and digitization and their impact on Indiana's labor market. Many of these trends existed before, but the events of recent years have escalated the misalignment in the Indiana labor market."[2]

Indiana's talent shortages have worsened and are expected to increase with an aging generation, slowing population growth, low labor participation rates, and evolving labor market needs.[3] By 2031, 72 percent of jobs in the United States will require education or training beyond high school.[4] Indiana faces a shortfall in meeting this demand.[5]

Declining education rates, underemployment and inadequate skills development impact both employers who are unable to find the talent they need to grow their businesses and the individuals who are unprepared for good jobs and are rather left to take jobs with little opportunity for wage growth.

Fast forward from 2022 to 2024 with some positive news. At the end of 2023, companies here and around the world committed to locate or expand in Indiana, investing more than $28.7 billion. This included mega-deals with semi-conductor, battery and electric vehicle manufacturers as well as data centers. This emerging growth represents significant opportunities for Hoosiers, especially if we are successful in preparing the requisite talent.

Now let's fast forward to 2040 and consider the trends and challenges Indiana will face – through the lens of generations of workers and the technological advances transforming workplaces.

A SHIFTING DEMOGRAPHIC LANDSCAPE

Already, Indiana and the world are experiencing the baby boom retirement wave: by 2030, all boomers will be at least 65.[6] Baby boomers no longer make up the largest age group and have been surpassed by the 72.24 million millennials who were born from 1982 to 2000.[7] By 2040, millennials and Generation Z (born between 1997 and 2012) will make up a majority of the workforce. Generation X (born between 1965 and 1980) will be exiting, and Generation Alpha (born between 2010 and 2014) will be up and coming.

As new generations enter the workforce leading to 2040, employers will encounter new challenges. Generation Z has grown up in an environment impacted by a global pandemic, climate issues, social unrest and political uncertainty. They also have always had information at their fingertips that simplifies and streamlines their lives as well as connects them to the world.

Against this backdrop, Gen Z has developed a set of values, behaviors and expectations that are considerably different from the baby boom generation. According to research conducted by Roberta Katz, a former senior researcher at Stanford's Center for Advanced Study in Behavioral Sciences, Gen Z is seeking the following in their work experience:

- Work-life balance. As flexible work schedules become more commonplace, the lines between work and home life become less defined. Gen Z is focused on ensuring a clearer delineation between work and their personal lives.

- Collaboration and teamwork. Gen Z values working together with coworkers toward a common goal. They also value the ability to work with leadership to solve problems and make decisions.

- Value-based work environment. Gen Z wants to work for organizations that make an impact on the world and share concern for similar issues and causes.[8]

Generation Alpha is soon to enter the workforce and will have advanced technical abilities due to growing up in an age when advancements led by artificial intelligence are being deployed and reckoned with on the world stage.

In addition to generational changes, it is expected that by 2045 over 50 percent of the U.S. population will be diverse. Black and Asian populations are expected to rise, and Hispanic workers are predicted to account for 30 percent of the labor force by 2060.[9]

While employers adjust to new generations and greater diversity in the workforce, they will also encounter fewer workers. The annual rate of population growth is expected to slow, as well as workforce participation rates.[10] If these predictions come true, this could mean fewer Hoosiers contributing to the workforce. Chapter 2 of this book provides more detail on population trends that will impact Indiana's workforce.

DIGITAL ADOPTION ACROSS INDUSTRIES

According to TechPoint's report *Seismic Shifts in the Talent Pipeline*, digital transformation and automation in key industry sectors, including advanced manufacturing and logistics, agriculture, life sciences and healthcare, are driving record high demand for tech talent.[11] That demand is expected to grow in emerging technologies, including intelligent systems and automation, automation, cloud platforms, interconnected networks and big data.

A good example of the impact of the digital adoption shift can be seen in Indiana's manufacturing industry where digital adoption has taken off and is expected to increase as manufacturers look for ways to increase productivity, competitiveness and profitability. While this pivot to the greater use of technology has benefits, it also means that some jobs will be eliminated or significantly changed.

Clearly, the digital transformation is not limited to the manufacturing workforce, but rather will extend to all sectors of the economy. This new reality has a direct impact on the skills that are needed and will be valued. The combination of an inadequately prepared workforce and population declines should be a wake-up call for employers and educators.

As we lean into the changes that are coming with a new demographic landscape and a technological revolution, the challenges we face become more evident and the need to address them more urgent. We must reimagine how we prepare for jobs that are changing and how we establish workplaces that address new ways of working.

CHALLENGE: PREPARING TALENT FOR NEW ROLES AND JOBS THAT DON'T EVEN EXIST YET

The years leading to 2040 will be marked by a shrinking workforce growth and technological advances that are critical to ensure economic growth. With technology changes at warp speed, it's difficult to predict the exact skill sets needed for the future workforce.

We will see workers approaching their careers differently and employers adjusting how they train and retain their workforce. Job hopping has always been a part of a worker's psyche. It has been about better earning potential, work environment or the boss. The U.S. Bureau of Labor Statistics shows that baby boomers held an average of 12.7 jobs from the age of 18 through 56, with half of those jobs held from 18 to 24.[12] Gallup reports that millennials and Gen Z change jobs more than older generations.[13] All predictions indicate that this trend will continue and challenge the retention of employees.

Moving toward 2040, personal preferences in jobs and roles will continue to matter, but it is also clear that career decisions will increasingly be a by-product of technology. The workforce of the future will need to focus on continual learning more than any prior generation. Gallup also reports that these younger generations have a strong desire to learn and grow in their careers, which is good news as jobs and roles change.

While employees are adjusting to new roles, employers must invest in reskilling and upskilling their workforce. For companies to retain talent during technology growth and remain competitive, employers will need to offer either in-house development or provide upskilling and education in partnership with postsecondary partners.

According to a Microsoft workplace survey by McKinsey & Company, 52 percent of Gen Z respondents said they were considering leaving their current jobs. However, if given the opportunity to change roles internally, 73 percent said they would stay, further supporting the role reskilling and upskilling will have in 2040.[14]

To that end, it will be important for educators, both at the K-12 and higher education levels, to instill a continuous learning mindset for students. K-12 education is foundational to ongoing development and career exploration. While much of this is occurring now, high school redesign should embrace high quality work-based learning experiences that teach both skills and resiliency (see Chapter 3).

Likewise, higher education should ensure career relevant experiences in all degrees and programs by working with employers to make these experiences available and valuable. This collaboration helps to meet the expectations of all three partners: students, educators and employers.

CHALLENGE: A NEW GENERATION OF WORKERS REQUIRES RETHINKING HOW WORK IS DONE

With the current and evolving labor market needs and flat population projections, employees will have more leverage in employment decisions and employers will need to develop a supportive workplace culture. For example, younger workers came of age in a digital environment with expectations for instant knowledge. Gen Z and Gen Alpha expect access to technology to be seamless, fast and uninterrupted.[15]

As noted earlier, a younger workforce values opportunities for connection and communication among their peers and their leaders. Research finds that Gen Z will work hard given flexibility in their work schedules and seek opportunities and support from their employer to advance professionally and learn new skills.[16] Understanding the specific skills needed to succeed in a career is important to this generation and could be translated by employers into on-the-job training, skills training and further educational pathways.

While adapting to generational work expectations, it will also be important for employers to grow the workforce by engaging specific groups of the adult population who are in various stages of transition. This speaks to the need for friendlier on-ramps for those adults who are returning to the workforce and incentives for those who choose to remain working in high-need areas until they are older. This outreach to specific groups of the adult population should include second-chance Hoosiers who were released from the correctional system, returning service members and foreign-born individuals. While the backgrounds of these groups are markedly different, the need for simplified and targeted strategies for employment is common among them.

CONCLUSION

In considering where, how and why people work, we should learn from our past to give us a clear path toward the future. What has caused our shrinking workforce participation rate and what factors can improve it? How do we build a workforce culture that better meets employees' expectations and employers' needs? How do we skill and reskill people so they are prepared for work and economic advancement? The answer to these and other questions can ensure growth opportunities for the future, personal prosperity and a stronger Indiana economy. ∎

ABOUT ASCEND INDIANA

Ascend Indiana was formed in 2016 as Central Indiana Corporate Partnership's cross-sector initiative focused on talent development. Over the years, the organization has played a leadership role in helping corporate, higher education, government and philanthropic partners address the state's talent needs. Specifically, Ascend connects young professionals with Indiana career and internship opportunities, provides consulting services to companies to meet their high-demand workforce needs and delivers research that enables systems-level change that positively impacts individuals throughout Indiana.

CHAPTER NOTES

[1] "Indiana's Evolving Labor Market Full Report." Ascend Indiana and EmployIndy. November 2022. https://ascendindiana.com/resources/indianas-evolving-labor-market-full-report-2022.

[2] "Indiana's Evolving Labor Market." Ascend Indiana and EmployIndy. November 2022.

[3] "Indiana's Evolving Labor Market." Ascend Indiana and EmployIndy. November 2022.

[4] "After Everything: Projections of Jobs, Education, and Training Requirements through 2031." Georgetown University Center on Education and the Workforce. November 2023. https://cew.georgetown.edu/cew-reports/projections2031.

[5] "College-Going Dashboard." Indiana Commission for Higher Education. Retrieved November 2023. https://www.in.gov/che/college-readiness-reports.

[6] "By 2030, All Baby Boomers Will Be Age 65 or Older." United States Census Bureau. December 10, 2019. https://www.census.gov/library/stories/2019/12/by-2030-all-baby-boomers-will-be-age-65-or-older.html.

[7] "U.S. population by generation 2022." Statista. https://www.statista.com/statistics/797321/us-population-by-generation.

[8] Melissa De Witte interview with Roberta Katz. "8 ways Gen Z will change the workforce." *Stanford Report.* February 14, 2024. https://news.stanford.edu/stories/2024/02/8-things-expect-gen-z-coworker.

CHAPTER NOTES (cont.)

9 Stephanie Ferguson, Jenna Shrove, and Isabella Lucy. "Data Deep Dive: The Workforce of the Future." U.S. Chamber of Commerce. October 4, 2023. https://www.uschamber.com/workforce/data-deep-dive-the-workforce-of-the-future.

10 Mitra Toossi. "A look at the future of the U.S. labor force to 2060." U.S. Bureau of Labor Statistics. September 2016. https://www.bls.gov/spotlight/2016/a-look-at-the-future-of-the-us-labor-force-to-2060/home.htm.

11 Ting Gotee et al. "Seismic Shifts in the Talent Landscape: 2023 TechPoint Indiana Tech Workforce Report." TechPoint. January 2023. https://techpoint.org/wp-content/uploads/2023/01/2023-TechPoint-Tech-Workforce-Report.pdf.

12 "Number of Jobs, Labor Market Experience, Marital Status, and Health for Those Born 1957-1964." Bureau of Labor Statistics. August 22, 2023. https://www.bls.gov/news.release/pdf/nlsoy.pdf.

13 Amy Adkins. "Millennials: The Job-Hopping Generation." *Gallup Business Journal.* 2016. https://www.gallup.com/workplace/231587/millennials-job-hopping-generation.aspx.

14 Sarah Skinner. "Mind the Gap." McKinsey & Company. October 2022. https://www.mckinsey.com/~/media/mckinsey/email/genz/2022/10/04/2022-10-04b.html.

15 Ravi Swaminathan. "Gen Zers are making their mark in the workplace – here are 4 things they expect." World Economic Forum. September 22, 2022. https://www.weforum.org/agenda/2022/09/the-4-expectations-gen-z-teams-have-workplace-future.

16 Kathy Bloomgarden. "Gen Z and the end of work as we know it." World Economic Forum. May 19, 2022. https://www.weforum.org/agenda/2022/05/gen-z-don-t-want-to-work-for-you-here-s-how-to-change-their-mind.

10

Predictions, Recommendations and a Call to Action

By Teresa Lubbers and Jacob Baldwin
Sagamore Institute

INTRODUCTION

This final chapter of *Workforce 2040: Pathways to Prosperity* synthesizes the insights and predictions presented throughout the book, offering a cohesive vision for Indiana's future. Building on the foundational work of the preceding chapters, we will not only revisit some of the key forecasts but also introduce new predictions that have emerged from our comprehensive analysis. This chapter is intended to provide actionable recommendations that Indiana's leaders can implement to foster a resilient and prosperous state.

The future of work, the future of workforce, and the future of learning are inextricably linked. These domains influence and shape each other in profound ways. Indiana's ability to effectively invest in all three areas can build a foundation for a dynamic future-informed economy. Understanding this interconnectedness is crucial for devising strategies that can effectively address the multifaceted challenges and opportunities ahead.

Effective preparation for the future economy is predicated on a firm understanding of the interrelated dynamics among the future of work, workforce and learning. The evolution of one aspect inherently influences the others. For instance, advancements in technology and changes in job markets demand a corresponding shift in educational paradigms to prepare the workforce adequately. Similarly, an adaptable workforce capable of flourishing in new work environments and industries is essential for sustained economic growth, but learning systems must first continuously evolve to equip people with learning agility capabilities and relevant skills. All three of these foundational facets of Indiana must be strong in order to build the future we want in Indiana.

Figure 10-1. The intersection of the future of work, workforce and learning in Indiana will define our prosperity

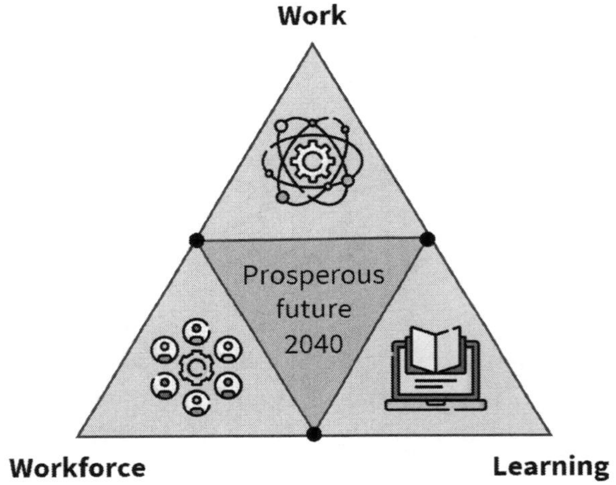

By delving into these areas, we aim to provide a roadmap that not only addresses immediate concerns but also anticipates future challenges and opportunities. Our goal is to inspire bold reforms that can lead to a thriving economy for all Hoosiers. As we look ahead, it is our hope that this chapter will serve as a catalyst for thoughtful action and sustained progress, guiding Indiana toward a prosperous 2040 and beyond.

THE FUTURE OF WORK

The future of work in Indiana will be defined by the state's ability to foster and attract dynamic, high-growth firms. Central to this vision is cultivating a robust culture of entrepreneurship and innovation and ensuring access to middle and higher-level growth capital. The creation of more startups hinges on a state policy environment conducive to technological innovation and taking advantage of federal opportunities, like the CHIPS and Science Act.

Key Challenges and Predictions

1. **Leveraging New Technologies** - Indiana's economic trajectory will heavily depend on its approach to emerging technologies. An aggressive stance toward deploying new tech tools can position the state as a leader in innovation, while complacency risks relegating the workforce to low-wage, low-skill jobs. The future will likely involve intense human-machine cooperation, emphasizing the continued relevance and centrality of human labor.

2. **Employee-Centric Labor Market** - Successful employers of the future will focus on becoming more employee-centric, recognizing that workplace flexibility and quality of place will matter more than ever. Creating environments that attract and retain talent will be crucial for sustained economic growth. Key quality of place amenities include strong educational options, affordable healthcare and housing, functional infrastructure, public safety, culture and recreation opportunities, and a sense of community.

Strategic Recommendations

To address these challenges and capitalize on opportunities, Indiana must adopt strategies that promote entrepreneurship and innovation.

1. **Promote Entrepreneurship and Growth Capital** - Ensure access to middle and higher-level growth capital to support startups and high-growth firms. Also, encourage public-private partnerships, particularly in science and technology hubs, to advance research and innovation. Furthermore, expand policies that foster a culture of entrepreneurship in young people and aspiring innovators through work-based learning experiences in schools and places of employment.

2. **Optimize Tax Policies** - Evaluate and reform Indiana's tax structure to make it more attractive for entrepreneurs and startups. Similarly, analyze the balance of property, sales, and income taxes to understand their impact on business attraction, growth and competitiveness.

3. **Enhance Educational and Training Systems** - Expand access to flexible skill development vehicles, including Indiana's Career

Scholarship Accounts, which provide a personalized, consumer-centric complement to traditional education and training programs. Ensure that education and learning systems are designed to offer digital and high-tech skill training while also embedding career-relevant experiences in all higher education degrees, programs and credentials. Promote employer engagement to reskill people through the state's employer training and workforce grant programs. Also, wherever possible, take advantage of every opportunity to consolidate, simplify and streamline the ever-expanding array of state-supported workforce training programs to make it easier for employers and individuals alike to navigate, utilize and benefit from these offerings.

4. **Leverage Federal Opportunities** - Take full advantage of federal legislation like the CHIPS and Science Act to boost the semiconductor industry and other high-growth sectors in Indiana. Encourage the development of tech hubs that facilitate public-private partnerships and advance research beneficial to startups. Additionally, position our research institutions, companies, and public-private partnerships to compete for funding from federal institutions, especially the National Institutes of Health and National Science Foundation.

5. **Utilize Creative Storytelling and Major Events** - Promote Indiana's entrepreneurial successes and innovative projects through creative storytelling directed to Hoosiers. Highlighting individual and organizational achievements can inspire and attract other potential entrepreneurs and investors, fostering a culture of innovation and ambition. Position Indiana as a premier destination for out-of-state entrepreneurs and businesses through strategic marketing campaigns tied to these events. Emphasize the state's business-friendly environment, quality of life, and support for innovation to attract talent and investment. Finally, leverage significant convenings such as Elevate Ventures' Rally conference that can serve as platforms for networking, attracting national and international attention, and forging influential relationships that drive economic growth.

Indiana's ability to navigate the future of work will significantly impact its economic success. By fostering entrepreneurship, optimizing tax policies, enhancing educational systems, and leveraging federal opportunities, the state can create a thriving, innovative work environment. These efforts will ensure that Indiana remains competitive and prosperous, providing a high quality of life for its residents as we approach 2040 and beyond.

FUTURE OF WORKFORCE

Indiana stands on the precipice of significant demographic shifts that will alter norms that have existed for decades. Unprecedented aging and a dwindling youth population will eventually upset consumption patterns and result in a shrinking workforce. Also, the diversity of our residents will continue increasing. These trends highlight the need for strategic planning to ensure a robust workforce capable of meeting future demands. As we look ahead, competition for prime-age workers will intensify, and the alignment between opportunity, personal well-being, and job preparedness will become increasingly critical.

Key Challenges and Predictions

1. **Slowing Population Growth and Demographic Shifts** - Indiana will experience a slowing population growth rate and an increasingly older and diverse population. Different regions of the state will experience these changes more acutely. These realities will necessitate a proactive approach to workforce development and retention.

2. **Competition for Prime-Age Workers** - The competition for workers aged 25-54 will become more intense as the workforce shrinks relative to demand. This demographic is crucial for economic stability and growth, making it imperative for Indiana to attract and retain these workers through innovative policies and initiatives. This challenge will be exacerbated by the tax burden these prime-age workers will shoulder as earlier generations live longer.

3. **Preparation for Future Jobs** - The imperative for connection between opportunity, personal well-being, and job preparedness will strengthen. Ensuring that individuals are equipped with the skills and knowledge required for future job markets will be essential for both personal and state-wide economic prosperity.

Strategic Recommendations

To address these challenges, Indiana must adopt a multifaceted approach including family-friendly policies, smart population growth strategies and other initiatives that enhance workforce participation.

1. **Encouraging Family-Friendly Policies** - Implementing policies that support families can significantly impact workforce participation. This includes ensuring affordable and high-quality education, housing and childcare. Paid family leave, tax credits, and public safety can also play a crucial role in making Indiana an attractive place for family formation and raising children. Government policies and private investments should ensure there is sufficient housing supply to keep prices affordable for families of all income levels. Development should include a plurality of dwelling types and not be limited to single-family dwellings only.

2. **Enacting Smart Population Growth Strategies** – Growing Indiana's population is vital to mitigate the worst effects of the coming demographic cliff and bolster the workforce. This includes policies that encourage both domestic and international migration of students and professionals. It is especially critical to grow the number of prime age workers who choose to stay or move to the state because of career options. Individuals who have connections to the Midwest or an employer are most likely to choose Indiana as their home. Cultivating employer connections and leveraging global ties will help position Indiana as a welcoming and opportunity-rich state.

3. **Building on Higher Education Assets** - Indiana's higher education institutions attract talent from other states and around the world. Our challenge is keeping these talented people in Indiana. We rank 36th in the country for the attraction and retention of college graduates. We need graduates to remain in Indiana and contribute to our economy, and one of the best ways to make that happen is to embed quality work-based experiences and internships into their educational pathways. By partnering with employers, our higher education system can ensure that graduates are prepared for good jobs that increase the likelihood that they will stay in the state.

4. **Reimagining the Earned Income Tax Credit (EITC)** - Expanding and reimagining the EITC can provide a significant boost to low-wage workers, helping them step out of poverty toward economic security. This approach not only supports individual dignity and generational wealth creation but also enhances overall workforce participation. It is worth exploring if Indiana can expand its state EITC to make it more generous, thereby supporting those in undervalued jobs. Also, as discussed in Chapter 2, Indiana should comprehensively evaluate its tax policies to ensure they are future-informed and competitive.

5. **Leveraging the Manufacturing Renaissance** - The state's strong manufacturing heritage coupled with advancements in hard-tech and manufacturing technologies provide a unique platform to improve labor force participation rates. For example, Indiana companies could employ more men who have been displaced by the decline in traditional manufacturing jobs or have simply stopped or never started working. Programs that offer retraining and upskilling in modern manufacturing techniques, as well as initiatives that winsomely highlight the evolving nature of "making things" can reinvigorate workforce participation. This approach not only taps into Indiana's industrial strengths but also addresses the socioeconomic challenges faced by people who are distanced from the labor market.

Indiana's ability to navigate these challenges and seize opportunities will determine its economic future. By implementing family-friendly policies, adopting population growth strategies, leveraging higher education assets, and reimagining our tax policies, Indiana can build a resilient workforce ready to meet the demands of 2040 and beyond.

THE FUTURE OF LEARNING

The landscape of education and learning is evolving rapidly, driven by technological advancements and shifting workforce demands. Indiana's existing education and training infrastructure must be more effective in preparing individuals for the future. As new options for learning emerge, opportunities for personalization and varied educational settings will become increasingly prominent. To thrive in this changing environment, learning providers must better align education with workforce needs and foster a culture of lifelong learning.

Key Challenges and Predictions

1. **Inadequate Existing Infrastructure** - The current education and training systems in Indiana are insufficient to meet the demands of the future workforce. Significant reforms and innovations are necessary to bridge this gap and equip individuals with skills that will be relevant in the future.

2. **Proliferation of Learning Options** - The future will see an expanding and sometimes confusing array of formal and informal learning opportunities and credentials. Personalized learning experiences will become more essential for both the individual learners and providers.

3. **Evolving Needs of the Future Economy** - Employers will need to identify and regularly update educators and policymakers about their requisite talent needs. Workers will need to develop learning agility skills and commit to lifelong learning to stay competitive in an ever-changing job market.

Strategic Recommendations

To address these challenges and leverage emerging opportunities, Indiana must implement several strategic initiatives.

1. **Develop a Navigation System and Intermediaries** - Create a comprehensive and simplified navigation system to guide individuals through the multitude of learning options available. This system should include intermediaries who can help train and retrain people, ensuring they acquire the skills needed for good jobs. In addition, curate quality insights and perspectives about how the economy will change. Facilitate engagement from individuals, learning providers, policymakers and employers to maximize preparedness for a changing and uncertain future. These relationships can allow the state to develop and publicize a regularly updated and actionable index of future-aligned, employment paths and skillsets.

2. **Ensure Quality of All Learning Providers** - Establish robust
    mechanisms to ensure the quality of all education providers.
    Accreditation should not be the sole measure of quality; other
    metrics, such as learner outcomes and employability, should also be
    put in place. For example, better utilize prior learning assessments
    to acknowledge the work experiences and knowledge gained by
    adult learners, so that their path to a credential or good job is
    simpler. Further, implement standards and best practices for
    evaluating the effectiveness of various learning platforms and
    providers, ensuring they meet the needs of both learners and
    employers. Improve data transparency in degrees and credential
    outcomes, including employment rates and earnings.

3. **Foster Collaboration Through a State Entity That Convenes All
    Stakeholders** - Increase the Governor's Workforce Cabinet's (GWC)
    effectiveness in bringing together public, private, and philanthropic
    sectors to collaboratively address future educational and workforce
    needs. This body should not only consider current needs but
    steadfastly advocate for forward-thinking strategies and policies in
    all parts of Indiana's economy. Ensure the State's convening entity
    has the necessary authority and resources to implement its vision,
    preserving its mission of aligning education with workforce
    requirements.

4. **Blur the Lines Between Working and Learning** - Promote
    initiatives that integrate work and learning, such as
    apprenticeships, internships and co-op programs. These initiatives
    should provide practical experience while individuals are still in
    school, making education more relevant and directly applicable to
    future careers. Similarly, encourage employers to adopt flexible
    learning models that allow employees to continuously upskill and
    reskill while working. As Jamie Merisotis, president of Lumina
    Foundation writes, "In today's world, frequent reskilling is the only
    way to stay ahead of the game."[1]

5. **Innovate in Early Childhood, K-12 and Higher Education** - Invest
    in meta-level data systems that measure readiness and quality from
    preschool through higher education. Reform education to provide
    more technology and personalized learning approaches. Focus on
    developing critical thinking and problem-solving skills alongside

digital literacy. Use technology to enhance teaching and learning to ensure that students are not left behind. Innovations such as AI tutors can offer a scalable solution and address learning obstacles and barriers to success.

Indiana's ability to innovate and adapt its education systems will play a pivotal role in shaping its economic future. By developing navigation systems, ensuring the quality of all learning providers, fostering collaboration, integrating work and learning, and reforming education, Indiana can build a robust and dynamic learning ecosystem. These efforts will prepare individuals for the challenges and opportunities of the future, driving sustained economic growth.

INDIANA'S FUTURE

Indiana stands at a critical juncture, and the decisions we make now will shape our state's future for decades to come. *Workforce 2040: Pathways to Prosperity* offers a comprehensive roadmap to navigate the challenges and seize the opportunities in work, workforce and learning. Now, it is time to act with a sense of urgency and purpose. Our collective efforts, led by visionary and bold leadership, must foster a culture of innovation and proactive adaptation across all sectors.

Public, private and philanthropic leadership must be aligned and committed to a shared vision. Building a culture that values entrepreneurship is essential. A commitment to continuously adapt, learn, and improve will position Indiana as a leader and provider for personal prosperity. Business leaders must take responsibility for offering lifelong growth opportunities for employees, especially in sectors most disrupted by technology. Educators and government leaders must reject complacency and engage with forward-thinking employers who have irreplaceable perspectives on the workforce needs of the future economy. The future of our workforce depends on re-engaging prime-age workers, leveraging our manufacturing renaissance, and promoting family-friendly policies and smart population growth strategies. The continued competitiveness of our human life sciences and ag-biosciences hubs demands greater investment and workforce depth. We need more high-growth firms, a more comprehensively robust ecosystem for startups and more alignment between our educational and training systems with the requirements of the future economy.

Success requires regular evaluation and adaptation. We will periodically revisit these recommendations and targets to measure progress and adjust our recommendations accordingly. Metrics such as household median income, labor force participation rates, population growth, education rankings, and the number of high-growth firms will help us gauge our progress. Every decision made by policymakers, business leaders, and educators should be guided by a critical question: "Are we taking bold enough steps to ensure future success?" This future-focused lens will help us prioritize actions that promote sustained prosperity and growth.

In this spirit, please share your thoughts and feedback on *Workforce 2040: Pathways to Prosperity* as well as your perspective on the most important issues affecting Indiana's future economy using the following QR code. We are eager to engage with you and your perspectives.

This book represents our best attempt to create awareness about the future and provide a framework for ongoing collaboration. Sagamore Institute will continue to convene leaders and stakeholders to review progress, share insights, and refine our strategies. By maintaining this commitment, we can help Indiana remain focused on the key future issues that will affect the paths to prosperity for Hoosiers in communities across the state.

Our efforts will ensure Indiana remains competitive and prosperous, providing a high quality of life for those who live here. Let us together create a legacy of success that will benefit generations to come. Now is the time to act boldly and decisively – Indiana's future will be shaped by our actions today. ∎

CHAPTER NOTES

[1] Jamie Merisotis. "For College Students – And For Higher Ed Itself – AI Is A Required Course." *Forbes*. July 17, 2024. https://www.forbes.com/sites/jamiemerisotis /2024/07/17 /for-college-students-and-for-higher-ed-itself-ai-is-a-required-course.

List of Figures

Made in the USA
Middletown, DE
09 September 2024

60684503R00104